MYTHOLOGY OF THE ZODIAC

MYTHOLOGY OF THE ZODIAC
TALES OF THE CONSTELLATIONS

MARIANNE McDONALD

MetroBooks

MetroBooks

An Imprint of Friedman/Fairfax Publishers

Library of Congress Cataloging-in-Publication Data available upon request.

ISBN 1-56799-581-0

Editor: Nathaniel Marunas
Art Director: Jeff Batzli
Designer: Paul Taurins
Photography Editor: Sarah Storey
Production Manager: Camille Lee

Color separations by Bright Arts Graphics (S) Pte. Ltd.
Printed in China by Leefung-Asco Printers Ltd.

10 9 8 7 6 5 4 3 2 1

For bulk purchases and special sales, please contact:
Friedman/Fairfax Publishers
Attention: Sales Department
15 West 26th Street
New York, NY 10010
212/685-6610 FAX 212/685-1307

Visit our website:
http://www.metrobooks.com

THE FIRST IMAGE IN EACH SECTION OF THIS BOOK,

EXCEPT FOR THE MILKY WAY SECTION, FEATURES ZODIACAL FIGURES

TAKEN FROM A BREATHTAKING FIFTEENTH-CENTURY ITALIAN BOOK

OF HOURS. (PIERPONT MORGAN LIBRARY, NEW YORK CITY)

ACKNOWLEDGMENTS

Heartfelt thanks to Alexander Cockburn, James Diggle, George Huxley,
Thomas MacCary, Nathaniel Marunas, Bridget McDonald, and Zeno Vendler
for their assistance in bringing this book to life

≈Contents≈

Our birth fate rules what we do.

Pindar, Nemean Ode V

We need not feel ashamed of flirting with the Zodiac. The Zodiac is well worth flirting with.

D.H. Lawrence

The twelve signs of the Zodiac tell us the limits of the night. Zeus already showed them to us all over the sky so that they could reveal the great year: the times to plow the new field, and the seasons to plant. So also on the sea, many sailors have predicted fierce storms, remembering the grim Arcturus, or other stars that come from ocean in the early morning or in early night. The sun, indeed, goes through all the signs throughout the year, as he drives his furrow, and he approaches now one, now another, or as he rises or as he sets, and another star sees another dawn.

Aratus, Phaenomena

Look you, Doubloon, your Zodiac here is the life of man in one round chapter.... To begin: there's Aries, or the Ram—lecherous dog, he begets us; then, Taurus, or the Bull—he bumps us into the first thing; the Gemini, or the Twins—that is, Virtue and Vice; we try to reach Virtue, when lo! comes Cancer the Crab, and drags us back; and here, going from Virtue, Leo, a roaring Lion, lies in the path—he gives a few fierce bites and surly dabs with his paw; we escape, and hail Virgo, the virgin! that's our first love; we marry and think to be happy for aye, when pop comes Libra, or the Scales—happiness weighed and found wanting; and while we are very sad about that, Lord! how we suddenly jump, as Scorpio, or the Scorpion, stings us in the rear; we are curing the wound, when whang come the arrows all round; Sagittarius, or the Archer, is amusing himself. As we pluck out the shafts, stand aside! here's the battering-ram, Capricornus, or the Goat; full tilt, he comes rushing, and headlong we are tossed; when Aquarius, or the Waterbearer, pours out his whole deluge and drowns us; and, to wind up, with Pisces, or the Fishes, we sleep.

Herman Melville, Moby Dick

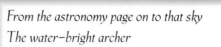

If Jupiter and Saturn meet,
What a crop of mummy wheat!

The sword's a cross; thereon He died:
On breast of Mars the goddess sighed.

Yeats, "Conjunctions,"
A Full Moon in March

From the astronomy page on to that sky
The water-bright archer
Swung up with those bells
And hung. Bell, water, star,
The handselled florin in my pocket,
All shone in the dark; the future's wages.
Eternity seemed boyish and the stars
Like wild oats, sown all over.

Seamus Deane,
"Send War in Our Time, O Lord," History Lessons

Till the charts and notes come crawling to life again
under a Night seething with
soft incandescent bombardment!

At the dark zenith a pulse beat,
a sperm of light separated wriggling
and snaked in a slow beam down
the curve of the sky, through faint
structures and hierarchies
of elements and things and beasts. It fell,
a packed star, dividing
and redividing until it was
a multiple gold tear. It dropped
toward the horizon, entered
bright Quincunx newly risen,
beat with a blinding flame and disappeared.

Thomas Kinsella, Vertical Man

Equal and opposite, the part that lifts
Into those full-starred heavens that winter sees
When I stand in Wicklow under the flight path
Of a late jet out of Dublin, its risen light
Winking ahead of what it hauls away:
Heavy engine noise and its abatement
Widening far back down, a wake through starlight...
Skies change, not cares, for those who cross the seas.

Seamus Heaney, "The Flight Path,"
The Spirit Level

INTRODUCTION

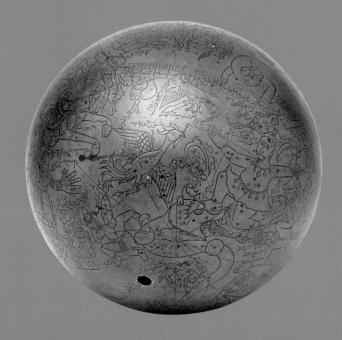

Astrology was considered a science by many ancient cultures: the Egyptians, the Babylonians, the Persians, the Greeks, the Romans, the Celts, the early and medieval Christians, and many others in one way or another took guidance from the stars. Man is destined to die, and so wants to relieve his fear of death and find out how best to live life. Thus we have projected our fears and desires onto the stars, thereby consulting a higher authority. It is a hallmark of sophisticated societies to find reference points in the stars for those mythological narratives that

ABOVE: There are many early star mappings, as illustrated by *Celestial Sphere* (1067), a brass globe engraved and inlaid with silver and black lac by Ziya al-Din Muhammad, Lahore, India. (Victoria and Albert Museum, London) RIGHT: *La Giustizia* ("Justice") is a painting by Giulio Romano (1499–1546) that illustrates Libra's driving principle, symbolized by the scales. (Vatican City, Rome)

frame their highest aspirations. The same celestial configurations are read differently by different peoples in different parts of the world and each culture has devised stories to satisfy deep human needs. In this way, the heavens are one of the principal sources of myth.

In some cases, perhaps, stargazing is as much an imposition of order, or meaning, as anything else. It is the belief that the stars rule our lives that prefigures a consultation of the heavens. And it is from that belief that comes the creation of myths. For instance, the Milky Way is a kind of international Rorschach test that tells us about the people who drew their stories from the sky. Norway's canon tells us that the Milky Way is a snowy street, but in African myth it is a river.

ASTRONOMY AND ASTROLOGY

Astronomy is the science of mapping the movements of the various planets and constellations. It measures and speculates about the universe as it shows the laws and customary movements of the various bodies. The etymology of the word "astronomy" is a combination of the Greek words for "star" and for "law," "custom," or "regulation." "Astrology" comes from the Greek words for "star" and for "word," "explanation," "reason," "computation," or "lore." So astronomy is the law of the stars, and astrology is

THIS IS A MARBLE BUST OF ZENO OF CITIUM (335–263 B.C.), THE FOUNDER OF THE STOICS, WHOSE PHILOSOPHY WAS INFLUENCED BY THE STARS. (MUSEO ARCHEOLOGICO, VENICE)

the lore. Astrology makes use of astronomy's measurements to predict future events or explain characteristics of individuals. Astrology developed coincidentally with astronomy and continued to be considered a sister science in the West until the seventeenth century. A ship's captain will use astronomy to plot his course; a ruler of a country, or a person seeking advice about her life, might consult astrology to determine a course of action.

The Babylonians are credited with making the first astronomical discoveries, around 3000 B.C. Already in the third millennium B.C., the Egyptians, based on information from the Babylonians and their own discoveries, could predict the rising of the Nile's waters from astronomical observations. The first instance of the zodiac in use may be attributed to the Babylonians (a text from 410 B.C. is said to be the earliest horoscope). Indeed, the Babylonians were the first to pick out the forms that we now know by the Latin names Gemini, Leo, Pisces, Taurus, and Scorpio. From the positions and "movements" of the stars, Egyptian and Babylonian astrologers predicted the fates of people and nations.

The Babylonians were the first to associate the gods with planets, giving them the names of their gods (in the West today, the planets are known by their Latin names). The

RIGHT, TOP:

PRESENTED HERE ARE FOUR OF THE TWELVE ANIMAL SIGNS OF THE CHINESE ZODIAC (PIG, OX, DRAGON, AND HORSE), FROM THE TANG DYNASTY, A.D. 618–906. (MUSEUM OF HISTORY, TAIPEI, TAIWAN) RIGHT, BOT-TOM: EGYPTIAN CONCEPTS ABOUT THE HEAVENS ARE FOUND IN THIS *ZODIAC OF DENDERAH*, FROM THE CEILING OF THE TEMPLE OF HATHOR, PTOLEMAIC PERIOD, 378–323 B.C. (LOUVRE, PARIS)

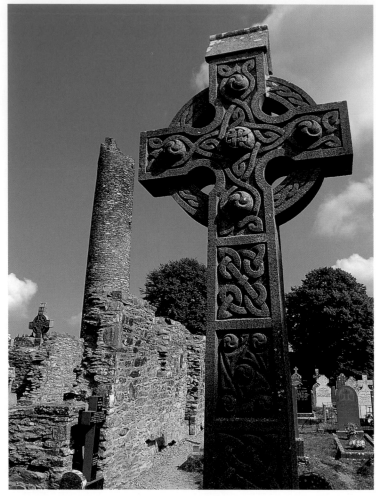

14

name of the most important Babylonian god, Marduk, was also the name of the most prominent planet (now called Jupiter, after the most powerful god of the Roman pantheon).

Hesiod, who lived sometime between 750 and 650 B.C., speaks of the birth of the universe in his *Theogony*, and in *Works and Days* provides an almanac of favorable and unfavorable days. His *Astronomia*, which gave the risings and settings of the constellations and possibly myths associated with them, only survives in a few fragments. Even Plato suggested that the sun, moon, stars, and

ABOVE, LEFT: THIS FRESCO BY SIMONE MARTINI (c.1280–1344) SHOWS EMPEROR JULIAN THE APOSTATE, WHO BELIEVED IN ASTROLOGY. (CHURCH OF SAN FRANCESCO, ASSISI) ABOVE, RIGHT: THIS CELTIC CROSS SHOWS THE SUN INTERWOVEN WITH THE CROSS. (MONASTERBOICE, IRELAND)

planets should be worshiped. But it was only after the western world's fascination with the Far East, brought closer by Alexander's conquests, that star worship really took hold among the Greeks. Eudoxus in the fourth century B.C. provides an account of some of the signs of the zodiac, and some of the names of the planets. Aratus (c. 315–240 B.C.) outlined more in his *Phaenomena*. A generation later, Eratosthenes provided the associated myths in the *Katasterismoi*, a work that was condensed by Pseudo-Eratosthenes, who wrote two to three centuries later. The Greek Stoics (300–150 B.C.) prized star lore as well. They believed that the universe was organized in a cosmic unity and developed a theory that human beings were governed by fate, and that their fates could be discerned by observing the universe, particularly the cycles of the stars and planets. The Persians also believed in astral influence, and according to Herodotus might have introduced some of their beliefs to the Greeks. Many other cultures also relied upon the science of astrology.

THIS BICCHERNA OF **1582** ILLUSTRATES THE GREGORIAN REFORM OF THE CALENDAR; IT SHOWS A SCHOLAR DISCUSSING THE CONSTELLATION SCORPIO. (STATE ARCHIVES, SIENA)

Astrology was also an important science in ancient Rome. In the first century A.D., for instance, it was a capital offense to cast the emperor's horoscope without his explicit authorization. Hyginus' *Poetica Astronomica* deals with some of the related lore. From the second century A.D. onward, Roman emperors were identified with the sun. Heliogabalus, the Roman emperor from 218 to 222 A.D., was in part named for the Persian sun god. The name Heliogabalus, or Elagabalus,

SCIPIO TVRAMINVS CRESCENTII FILIVS CV EVERIT MAGISTRATVS BICCHERNÆ CAMERARIVS TEMPORE QVO GREGORIVS XIII PONTIFEX MAXIMVS ANNO REFORMAVER IN PERPETVAM HVIVS REI MEMORIAM HANC TABOLA PINGERE FECIT

combines Greek ("helios," for the sun) and Persian (from the ancient Syrian deity Emesa) and means "Sun God."

The emperor Julian "the Apostate," whose life is brilliantly recounted in a modern novel by author and historian Gore Vidal, was a fierce defender of paganism and swore by astrology. Christian theology took a formal stand against astrology, but many Christians secretly practiced it. In much the same way that the pagan gods were associated with the sun, Christians took *Sun*day as their sacred day, identifying the sun with God. Remember that Christmas, December 25, was the old birthday of the sun, celebrated in pre-Christian communities (for instance, the *natalis invicti solis*, or "birthday of the invincible sun," according to the Mithraic religion popular in ancient Rome.)

Many comparable pagan festivals were celebrated at this time. The 25th was the day after the Roman Saturnalia, celebrated from December 17 to 24. The time of the winter solstice was regarded as magical, and Newgrange's shrine/tomb in Ireland (dating from around 3000 B.C., just as the Babylonians were making their discoveries) was designed to catch the sun's rays in the depths of its labyrinth on this very day. The Yule Feast celebrated in northern Europe commemorated the rebirth of the sun and the lengthening of days. There are Scandinavian legends centering on this time as well. Hanukkah, the festival of lights, is celebrated at this time, symbolically linking it with the period of the solstice. The lights on the Christmas tree may also derive from northern European associations.

OPPOSITE, TOP: THIS 1686 ENGRAVING BY ENGLISH ASTRONOMER PHILIP LEA SHOWS THE CONSTELLATIONS AS SEEN IN THE NORTHERN HEMISPHERE. OPPOSITE, BOTTOM: THESE ARE CONSTELLATIONS AND A STAR MAP FROM THE SO-CALLED *DÜRER MAP*, OF THE SOUTHERN CONSTELLATIONS, DESIGNED AND DRAWN BY ALBRECHT DÜRER AND PRINTED FROM A WOODBLOCK, CIRCA 1515. THE HIGHLY STYLIZED REPRESENTATION OF THE CONSTELLATION FIGURES HAD ALREADY BEEN ESTABLISHED BY THE EARLY SIXTEENTH CENTURY.

Celtic crosses typically show a circle behind the cross; this sun-symbol recalls the ancient Celtic god Lugh, whose name means "one who shines." Brian Friel's award-winning play, *Dancing at Lughnasa*, commemorates the yearly festival celebrated in Ireland in honor of Lugh, Lughnasa.

The Arabs, and the followers of Mohammed (570–632 A.D.), endorsed many of the traditional teachings of the astrologers, and made contributions of their own, interpreting conjunctions of planets in the various signs.

Astrology continued to be popular during the Byzantine period and the twelfth-century Spanish-Arab scholar Averroës considered it a science, as did the English Roger Bacon in the next century. In the sixteenth century, Pope Leo X established a chair of astrology at the University of Rome. Shakespeare's plays are riddled with astrological references, though he consistently makes belief in astrology a sign of a character's superstitious or backward nature. Elizabeth I had a private astrologer, John Dee. Many of the great astronomers, including Galileo and Kepler, were astrologers on the side.

Nevertheless, by 1650 belief in astrology was dwindling, victim of the seventeenth-century intellectual revolution associated with Galileo, Francis Bacon, and Descartes, among others. The eighteenth century was even less favorable to astrology, but it still survived as a "science." As soon as new planets were discovered (Uranus in 1781 and Neptune in 1846), their influences were incorporated into astrological lore. The Romantics of the nineteenth century were predictably more sympathetic to astrology. Poetry from the period abounds with astrological allusions.

17

Today, astrology is wildly popular. There is a London Faculty of Astrological Studies that is world-renowned. Daily astrological guides can be found in most grocery stores in the United States, and countless popular magazines carry a regular column on astrology.

THE CLASSICAL ZODIAC

The word *zodiac* derives from a Greek word that means "life," or "living creature." The English word *zoo* derives from the same root, as does *zoology*, the study of living creatures. The sun passes through twelve constellations, all named for living creatures (except the scales of Libra, which is a Roman invention) and located along the path of the ecliptic (an imaginary plane connecting the earth, sun, and solar system). (Of course, Earth really moves around the sun, but speaking about the sun as if it moves through the sky is an accepted convention when discussing the zodiac.) Another convention is the dates that bracket the sun's transit through a sign; these periods actually vary over time.

There are many classifications for the signs of the zodiac, corresponding to the constellations of the same name, arising from astrological interpretation. There are three earth signs, three air signs, three fire signs, and three water signs. Earth signs are said to get along with water signs, and fire

signs with air signs (after all, earth is made fertile with water's help, and air feeds fire). By the same token, signs associated with elements that don't mix (for instance, fire and water) are not supposed to be compatible. Nevertheless, if one lacks an element in one's chart, then someone who has a lot of that element may be a perfect complement to that person.

Of course, there are many other factors that go into compatibility between people, and into the interpretation of one's star chart. In casting a horoscope, it is essential to know the minute, hour, date, and location on the planet of birth to set up a chart. The time and place of birth tell the astrologer in what sign the Earth was; that sign is the ascendant, or rising sign. The astrologer also determines the positions of the other planets throughout the zodiac from the same information. (The sun and moon are considered planets.) The first house is determined by the ascendant, and the houses are numbered clockwise through twelve, overlaying the sequence of the twelve constellations. A person's chart is interpreted according to the placement of the planets and other heavenly bodies in these houses at the time of birth. A relationship is described by a comparison of two charts. No life or relationship is definitively good or bad, just as no person is. Instead, astrological information simply suggests tendencies. Even if

18

there were no validity to it, such information can offer a launching point for soul-searching or conversation between people.

There are six signs that are masculine, and six that are feminine. Gods rule each of the signs. There are many more classifications including interpretations of geometrical relationships of the planets to one another. These relations affect a person at the hour of birth and are said to shape the character permanently. By comparing present configurations in relation to a person's birth or natal chart, astrologers suggest answers to questions such as when a medicine will work, when one should marry, which days are dangerous or safe, and so forth.

THIS FANCIFUL SANSKRIT ZODIAC AND STAR MAP OF CIRCA **1840** IS CALLED *JEWEL OF ESSENCE OF ALL SCIENCES*. IT IS INTERESTING TO NOTE THE ABSENCE OF FIGURES FROM THE VEDIC, OR HINDU, TRADITION.

ZODIACS OF OTHER CULTURES

The Chinese have a zodiac of animals, each of which has influence over one year in a twelve-year cycle (this differs from the western zodiac, which features a different character for every month). The attributes of the particular animal (for instance, the rat or the monkey) are said to belong to the people born in that year. These attributes are not necessarily the attributes of a real animal, but as that animal is treated in the Chinese mythology. The rat, for instance, is the first sign because when the Buddha summoned all the animals the rat showed up first. Certain animals have particular affinities, such as rats with monkeys and dragons.

19

LEFT: This Chinese Buddhist *TANKA* shows the twelve animals of the zodiac and the eight sacred symbols of Buddhism (in the second circle). In the center, three animals illustrate the cyclical flow of nature.

OPPOSITE, TOP: Found in the Yucatan, this fourteenth-century illustration is from a Mayan fortune-telling calendar that predicted the good and bad days based on the positions of the stars and planets. (Museo de America, Madrid)

OPPOSITE, BOTTOM: This arresting diagram of a man shows which zodiacal symbols govern the various parts of the body, from Aries at the head to Pisces at the feet. (Trinity College, Cambridge, England)

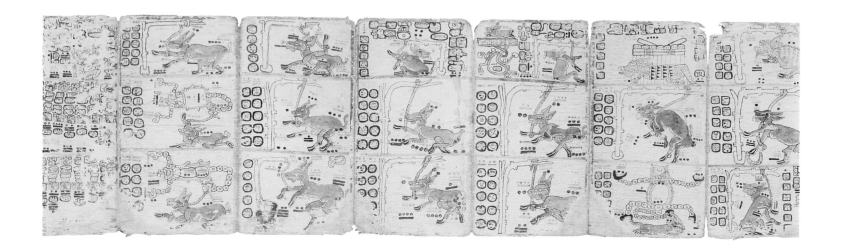

Early and medieval Christians assigned the names of the twelve apostles to the signs of the zodiac, and the Hebrews assigned the names of the twelve tribes.

The Zulu culture in Africa calls the zodiac Mulu-Mulu and claims that all the animals came from these stars: for instance, the lion from the lion, the bull from the bull, seals from Capricorn, and grain from Virgo, the Green Maiden. Thus did life come from the stars. There are thirteen signs in the Zulu zodiac. Those born under the sign of Umkhomo, the Whale (December 28 to January 6), are particularly blessed, and are expected to be servants of humanity.

CONCLUSION

Myths shape thought as well as provide explanations. They have been and continue to be a basis for literature and the stuff of epic. Myths were used to explain the stars and act as mnemonic devices so that a ship's pilot or traveler could remember a star formation. These stories reflected the culture in which they arose. Our reasoning faculty inspires us to seek order in the stars.

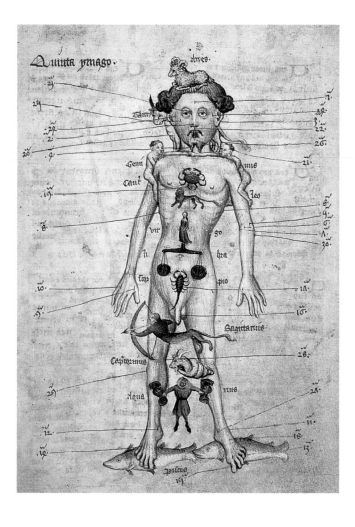

Told and retold, these tales evolved and changed, acquiring variants over time. This book is a guide to some of the many myths associated with the constellations of the zodiac as well as with the Milky Way. If astrologers are to be believed, the zodiac has an incredible influence over our lives. At the very least astrology provokes some fairly exciting discussion. The Milky Way is our home, our galaxy (a word that is derived from the Greek word for "milk"). For these reasons and more, this survey of the myths associated with these star groupings can tell us much about ourselves as well as about the different cultures of the world.

MYTHOLOGY OF THE ZODIAC
TALES OF THE CONSTELLATIONS

OPPOSITE: THIS COMPOSITE GRAPHIC BY WILLIAM LAW AFTER THE SEVENTEENTH-CENTURY WORK OF JACOB BÖEHME SHOWS THE ZODIACAL MAN AND WOMAN, SURROUNDED BY THE PLANETARY SYMBOLS, WITH THE PLANETARY INFLUENCES MARKED ON THEIR BODIES. THE SUN IS CLOSE TO THE HEART, AND THE MOON GOVERNS THE GENITALS.

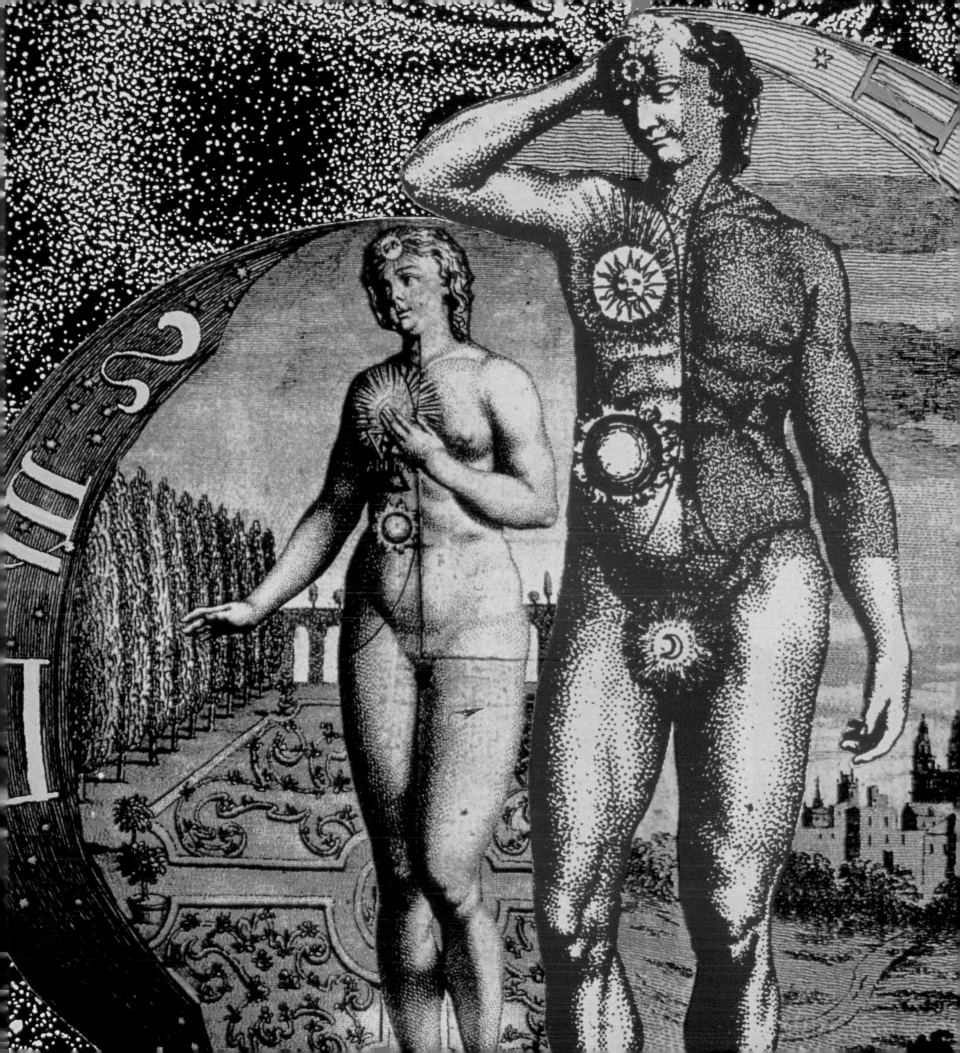

*Greybeards tell the story that Pan,
shepherd of the fields,
blew on his well–fitted reeds and
produced a sweet–sounding
song that echoed in the Argive
mountains. With this song, he
lured from its suckling mother a
lamb of rich golden fleece.*
—Euripides, Electra

*The best of men sought the golden
fleece.*
—Euripides, Medea

*The Ram venturing beyond the sea
serenely shines,
and leads the year, the ruler of all
the signs.*
—Manilius, Astronomica

24

A ries, the Ram, is the first sign of the Greek zodiac and is sometimes considered to represent Jason's golden fleece. The golden fleece may be directly associated with the ancient country of Colchis, on the Black Sea, commemorating the gold that came from there. (Interestingly, throughout ancient Greece and the Middle East, fleece was used in panning for gold; the gold particles would stick to the hairs, causing the fleece to shimmer in the light.)

The story of the golden fleece begins in Boeotia, where Athamas ruled. He was married

OPPOSITE: *JASON AND THE GOLDEN FLEECE*, BY THE FLEMISH MASTER ERASMUS QUELLINUS (1607–1678), DEPICTS THE HERO STEALING THE FLEECE FROM COLCHIS. IN THE HEAVENS, JASON IS REPRESENTED BY ARGO NAVIS AND THE FLEECE BY ARIES.

to a woman named Nephele, meaning "cloud." (This may be the same Nephele, or "cloud-woman," that Zeus created in the likeness of Hera, whom Ixion raped, thinking it was Hera. From this union issued the centaurs, a race of half-man, half-horse creatures. The most famous of these was Chiron, immortalized in some versions as Sagittarius.)

Hera watched over Nephele, her *altera ego*. Nephele gave Athamas two children, Phrixus and Helle, but the king abandoned her and married Ino, by whom he had Learchus and

Melicertes. Ino plotted to get rid of the first children in order to secure a position for her own brood. First, she burnt the corn seed that was planted so that nothing sprouted; then she bribed the Delphic oracle to say that Phrixus and Helle must be sacrificed to cure the blight. The children were brought to the altar, but Nephele, who had supernatural powers herself, caused a cloud to form and then whisked them away on a golden-fleeced ram that was to bring them to safety in Colchis.

During the journey, Helle fell off the ram; the sea in which she drowned is thus called the Hellespont. (Some identify Helle as a moon goddess, and her death is taken to symbolize the victory of the male sun god, with whom Aries is identified.) Phrixus married Chalciope, the daughter of Aeetes, a son of Helios and brother of Circe (the witch who turned Odysseus' crew into swine). Aeetes' other

ABOVE: THIS SIDE OF A SAR-COPHAGUS FROM NAPLES SHOWS ANOTHER VERSION OF JASON STEALING THE GOLDEN FLEECE FROM COLCHIS. OPPO-SITE: ARIES, FROM AN ENGLISH PSALTER, YORK, CIRCA 1170. (GLASGOW UNIVERSITY LIBRARY, GLASGOW)

daughter, Medea, also had magic powers. In Colchis, the golden ram was sacrificed, its gleaming fleece hung from a tree and guarded by a dragon that never slept.

This was the fleece that Jason later sought with the support of the goddesses Hera and Athena. Jason was commanded by Pelias, the king of Iolcus, to bring the fleece back to Greece. (Pelias hoped that this would be an impossible task: he wanted to get rid of Jason, who was claiming a share of the royal inheritance because Pelias' half-brother Aeson was Jason's father and Pelias had usurped his throne.) The ship was built by Argos, a son of Phrixus, who knew people in Colchis, where he was born. Jason collected an assemblage of heroes and they embarked on their quest.

When Jason, in the course of his search for the golden fleece, reached Colchis, Hera told Aphrodite to make the princess Medea fall in love with him, so that the sorceress would help the young hero perform certain tasks set him by Aeetes, her father. Protected by a magic ointment that Medea gave him, Jason yoked fire-breathing bulls. Then he plowed a gigantic field and sowed dragon's teeth, from which sprang soldiers. Jason threw a stone into their midst; this caused them to contest who had dealt the first blow and eventually they slew each other.

Jason then killed the dragon, which had been magically put to sleep by Medea, and took the golden fleece. Finally, he escaped with Medea and had various adventures en route from Colchis to Iolcus to Corinth. In the latter city, Jason abandoned Medea for a new princess. In vengeance, Medea slew the children she had had by Jason and escaped in a dragon-drawn chariot, a gift from her grandfather, the sun-god Helios.

Aries has also been identified with the golden ram, the ownership of which connoted kingship, which may have been a gift from Hermes to Atreus, the father of Agamemnon (later the leader of the assault on Troy). Thyestes, the brother of Atreus, challenged his kinsman's right to the throne of Mycenae. Thyestes seduced Aerope, Atreus' wife, whom he convinced to steal the ram for him. Thyestes flaunted the ram then in his possession and thus gained the throne. (In one version, Thyestes was given the kingship until the sun would set in the east. Zeus, exacting divine justice, made the sun reverse its course one day, and indeed the sun set in the east.)

Atreus subsequently regained his kingship, but he took a terrible vengeance on Aerope, throwing her from a cliff. He then exiled Thyestes. Under the pretext of a reconciliation with Thyestes, Atreus invited his brother to a feast at which he served up Thyestes' children to the unwitting father. At the end of the meal, Atreus produced the children's heads and divulged the contents of the stew. Thyestes then cursed the house of Atreus and departed.

Consulting the oracle of Delphi, Thyestes was told he would be avenged if he had a son by his one remaining daughter, Pelopia, who had been away when Atreus had seized her brothers. Thus was conceived Aegisthus, who seduced Clytemnestra, Agamemnon's wife. After he returned from Troy, Agamemnon was killed by Aegisthus abetted by Clytemnestra, in revenge for Atreus' crime. Clytemnestra had her own grievances to add to those of Aegisthus. First, there was Agamemnon's sacrifice of their daughter, Iphegenia, to get fair winds for his voyage to Troy. Second, he had been foolish enough to bring home Cassandra, princess of Troy, as his mistress.

Greek myths resemble modern soap operas in their infinite elaboration of episodes, but unlike the soaps, Greek myths are consistent in their attempts to work out all possible variations on a basic theme. They also resonate more truly with the inner nature—the deepest emotions and drives—of human beings, revealing the patterns of human experience. Their universal quality and haunting truths have ensured their survival.

The golden ram represented by Aries can be interpreted in several ways. Perhaps it is a symbol of private property and the inherent dangers of covetousness. Aries the constellation is ruled by Mars, the planet named for the god of war,

27

and is a fire sign. Fire can be life-giving, as it was when Prometheus presented it as a gift to man, or when it burned in the hearth of Hestia, fire-tender of the Greek gods. Fire can also be destructive, in the image of Mars: in modern terms, the fire of nuclear fission, Hiroshima's bane.

Peoples from the Euphrates Valley called the constellation of Aries *Gam*, "the scimitar," and it was said to protect the country against the Seven Evil Spirits, or the Spirit of the Tempest. Aries was also an important constellation for the

MARS BEING CROWNED BY VICTORY, BY PETER PAUL RUBENS (1577–1640). ON THE RIGHT ARE APHRODITE, EROS, AND THE DEFEATED SATYR. ARIES IS RULED BY MARS, THE PLANET NAMED FOR THE GREEK GOD OF WAR. (GEMÄLDEGALERIE, DRESDEN)

Egyptians because it reached its highest point at the same time that Sirius rose, which signaled the Nile's flooding. The Egyptians of the Ptolemaic period associated the constellation with Zeus Ammon, who had the head of a ram. When Dionysus was in Africa, a miraculous flying ram appeared and guided him to a place where he and his army could find water; in return, the god placed the ram among the stars. A temple was built to Zeus Ammon by the Egyptians at that spot, with a statue of the god, complete with ram's horns. The Ammon oracle in Egypt claimed that Alexander the Great was the son of Ammon, so many artists depicted this king with ram's horns (a tetradrachma from 300 B.C. shows Alexander as the god Ammon with ram's horns). Other myths say that Zeus himself took the form of a ram to hide from the giants when they attacked. The main star of the constellation is known to various Arab tribes as Hamal, from *Al-Ras al-Hamal*, meaning "The Sheep's Head."

The Zulus believe that people born under this sign are true warriors, although not necessarily leaders, and very loyal. One myth recounts that a black ram named Dushuza was immortalized as a constellation by the sun god because the ram saved the sun god's daughter. One day an ugly and malodorous giant saw the lovely Nozinyanga, the moon goddess and daughter of the sun god, bathing. Overwhelmed by the beauty of her naked body, the giant rushed toward her, rape in his heart. She fled into a mountain, which she caused to open and then close behind her, to escape his intended violence. Her father missed her desperately and the whole world suffered from her absence. To rectify the situation, God the Father, Unkulunkulu, sent Dushuza, a gigantic black ram, to break the mountain open and

THIS TURKISH PAINTING (1583) SHOWS AN ANGEL BRINGING THE RAM AS ABRAHAM IS ABOUT TO SACRIFICE ISHMAEL, OR ISAAC. THE RAM IS THE SUBSTITUTE FOR THE HUMAN SACRIFICE, AND REFLECTS A CHRISTIAN INTERPRETATION OF ARIES.

return the goddess to the world. The ram crashed against the mountain with all his might and split it open, revealing the goddess. But a rock slide marred half of her face, making it moon-shaped. It is said that if the earth is ever threatened, God the Father will again call on Dushuza for help.

The constellation is one of the twelve Chinese signs, the dog. The Chinese call two stars in the constellation of Aries *Leu*, "the trail of the dress," and the other *Oei*, "the belly." Along with the constellations Taurus and Gemini it is called the White Tiger, or the "lake of fullness," or "five reservoirs of heaven," and the "house of the five emperors."

Christian interpretations of the constellation vary, from Abraham's ram to God's own son, who was sacrificed to save humankind. When the sun was in this constellation, Josephus claimed, the Hebrew people gained their freedom from Egypt. It is identified with the tribe of Judah.

The Assyrians called this constellation *Lu-Hun-Ga*, "The Day Laborer," who is associated with Dumuzi, a provider of succulent dates. Dumuzi's wife, Inanna, is also associated with sweet dates. The early dawn appearance of this constellation signaled the time that the female date-palms must be fertilized—by hand, with pollen from the male plant—and the one

29

who accomplishes this important task is "the day laborer" of the constellation.

As we can see, this constellation is important in the yearly cycle of fertility. Since it is closely associated with the sun, it also fosters the growth of grain. As a harbinger of flooding it provides water.

Aries (March 21 to April 19) is a cardinal fire sign and is governed by Mars. Its plant is a rose, and its jewel is the scintillating diamond. The colors associated with it are orange and purple. People born under this sign are leaders, and pioneers; sometimes domineering, they can have violent tempers. They often have a need to be

THIS DETAIL FROM THE GHENT ALTARPIECE (1432) SHOWS THE "ADORATION OF THE LAMB," BY JAN VAN EYCK. THIS IS A RELIGIOUS INTERPRETATION OF THE SIGN OF ARIES. (CATHEDRAL ST. BAVO, GHENT, BELGIUM)

mothered. If their needs are satisfied, they can be most sensitive and caring. Here one finds talented artists, adventurers, explorers, soldiers, and athletes. They take risks, and are brave, loyal, and dedicated to universal causes. Aries are original, creative and freedom-loving people, sometimes passionate and impulsive, at other times selfish and foolhardy. Their energy is exceptional. Outstanding people of this sign are: Johann Sebastian Bach, Casanova, Charles Chaplin, James Diggle, Vincent van Gogh, Joseph Haydn, Seamus Heaney, Harry Houdini, Henry James, Sergei Rachmaninov, Leonardo da Vinci, and Emile Zola.

TAURUS

Ταῦρος

Dionysus: *He found a bull where he thought he had imprisoned me....*

Pentheus: *You seem to be a bull leading me, and to have grown horns on your head. Were you a beast before? Now you are really bullified!...*

Chorus [to Dionysus]: *Appear as a bull or many-headed dragon, or be seen as a lion blazing with flames.*
　　　　　　—Euripides, Bacchae

I like myself, but I won't say I'm as handsome as the bull that kidnapped Europa.
　　　　　—Cicero, De Natura Deorum

When bright Taurus with his golden horns opens the year, and the Dog falls, ceding to the opposing star so near.
　　　　　　—Virgil, Georgics

In time the savage bull doth bear the yoke.
　　　　—William Shakespeare, Much Ado About Nothing

That jewell'd mass of millinery, That oiled and curled Assyrian Bull.
　　　　—Alfred, Lord Tennyson, Maud

The Irish bull is always pregnant.
　　　　—Mahaffy, Oral Tradition

31

The constitution Taurus is associated with the Cretan Bull, which Heracles captured as one of his tasks. It may also be associated with the bull that carried Europa off, the disguise taken by Zeus on one of his amorous adventures; the bull that Pasiphaë loved; or the brazen-footed bulls that Jason had to slay. Some say that it is a cow, commemorating Io, Zeus' beloved, and the forebear of Heracles. Io resembles the Egyptian goddess Isis in having curved horns, a sign of the moon. The divine bull Apis is sometimes identified with Epaphus, whose name means "the touch," the son that Io bore to Zeus in Egypt, conceived when he touched her. The bull is a symbol of strength and potency, and its sacrifice in the spring helped ensure the fertility of the fields in many Mediterranean cultures. One can also associate the bull with the sun, and Europa with the moon, her abduction another installment of the patriarchal takeover. Dionysus frequently takes the form of a bull, as Euripides' *Bacchae* attests.

Two star clusters make up the figure of the bull, and these are the Hyades (generally considered five and located on the bull's face) and the Pleiades (generally considered seven and located on the bull's neck). Both groups are usually considered daughters of Atlas. Some Greeks claim the Hyades are the transformed daughters of Erechtheus, the

king of Athens who had to decide which god would be the patron of the city. Poseidon and Athena competed and offered their gifts: Poseidon struck a rock and a horse leaped out; Athena caused an olive tree to grow. Erechtheus chose the goddess.

Poseidon became angry, and caused his son Eumolpus to come from Thrace to attack Athens. Erechtheus received a terrible oracle that commanded him to kill one of his daughters to save the city. He obeyed, but her sisters could not bear to live without her, so they also gave their lives. Professor Joan Connelly, a classical archaeologist and art historian, has argued that theirs is the sacrifice represented on the great frieze of the Parthenon, the main temple dedicated to Athena in Athens. Athena rewarded these maidens for

OPPOSITE: *The Rape of Europa*, by Paolo Veronese. Zeus took the shape of a bull when he abducted Europa. (Palazzo Ducale, Venice)

ABOVE: *Bacchantes with a Dionysiac Bull.* Governed by Venus, Taurus is a sexy sign; it is hardly surprising, then, that a bull figured in various Dionysian rites. (Uffizi Gallery, Florence)

their bravery by immortalizing them as the Hyades. These beautiful stars on the head of Taurus are shaped in a V (which to Latin speakers perhaps stood for Venus, the governing planet). This cluster includes the bright reddish star Aldebaran, which in Arabic means "the next one" because it rose after the Pleiades. There are other names in Arabic, including "stallion" and "camel." Hindus called the cluster "red deer."

Another story is that the Hyades were nymphs who protected Zeus on Crete when he hid from his father, Cronus, who was trying to kill him. (A similar tale is told of the Pleiades.) For this service, Zeus elevated the nymphs to the stars. Still another version has it that they were nurses of the young Bacchus, or teachers of Bacchus when he was in India.

Another myth associates these stars with the sister of Hyas, who was killed by a boar as he was hunting. They weep forever, and thus signal rain, as they did in ancient Greece when they rose in autumn. Hyas is a double of Adonis and also of Osiris, and is a symbol of the fertile crop that is cut down only to be reborn.

A less reverent but equally ancient myth calls these stars pigs, probably because the rainy season creates mud, the beloved medium of pigs. Perhaps Aldebaran was the mother sow that watched over the others. The Roman term *suculae*, which could mean "little pigs," might not relate to *sus* ("pig") but to *sucus* ("juice"); thus, the stars might simply be the "little wet ones." This is what their name means in Greek, coming

THIS FIRST-CENTURY ROMAN MOSAIC, *EUROPA ON THE BULL*, AFTER A PAINTING BY ANTIPHILOS, SHOWS THE ABDUCTION OF EUROPA BY ZEUS, IN BULL FORM. (LANDESMUSEUM, OLDENBURG, GERMANY)

from *huein*, meaning "to rain." The time they rose in the fall signaled storms, and when they disappeared in spring, rain came. Claude Lévi-Strauss recounts stories about the Pleiades told by tribes in South America attesting to how the stars brought rain and how it was harder to find food when they were not present.

One romantic story from the Arabic tradition relates that Aldebaran courted Al Thurayya (the Pleiades), driving his camels before him to prove his wealth since she had rejected Aldebaran when he was poor. Hindus saw a wagon in these stars, and the Chinese saw a rabbit net, or *Yu Shi*, "the ruler of rain." Individual stars have the usual repertory of varied titles in the Chinese tradition, including "fire-carriage," "many princes," "heavenly gate," "heavenly street," and "heaven's festival."

According to the Zulus, people born under the sign of the Bull are very aggressive and boastful. They hate to be ignored. It seems that in the night sky there was a great white bull named Ntontozayo whom the god of the sun asked to watch his cattle. This bull loved to bellow and he would do it loudly every night, feeling that he was on top of the world, which, of course he was. His arrogance and pride increased daily. One night his boastful bellowing was at last answered by a formidable bull with six heads, three in front and three in back. It was Burumatara, the bull of the moon, also known as the bull who can break mountains apart.

Ntontozayo urinated from fear, and his fears proved to be warranted. Burumatara hurled him to the top of the universe and gored him when he landed on a passing planet. Ntontozayo lay very still, hoping Burumatara would think he was dead, but Burumatara trampled him some more, urinated on him, and deposited a huge pile of dung on his head. Then came the ultimatum. Burumatara then insisted Ntontozayo say that he was nothing more than a pile of dung, or he would kill him. The vain, now abject bull complied, and Burumatara told him the gods had

delegated him to teach Ntontozayo that age-old lesson: pride comes before a fall. Burumatara then urinated on Ntontozayo's head to clear the dung away. Ntontozayo is still the bull in the sky, but he has learned humility. It is said that the gods will send Burumatara to punish rulers and countries that act arrogantly.

The Sumerians called Taurus *mul-Is Li-E*, or "the bull's jaw," and this no doubt referred to the V-shaped Hyades. Similarly, some South American Indians also associated the stars that comprise the Hyades with the head of a bull, others with the jaw of an ox, and others still with a tapir's jaw. The Chinese say these stars form part of the constellation known as White Tiger, and then again *Ta Leang*, "the great bridge." This constellation was also important to the Druids, who held their Tauric festival when it appeared. The golden calf worshipped by the Hebrews may relate to this constellation as well.

The Pleiades, traditionally numbered at seven, are actually many more. Some counts include their mother and father, Atlas and Pleione, who figure in the handle of the Pleiad dipper. In antiquity their early-morning rising coincided with the spring harvest, and their evening appearance with the fall plowing, which prepared the ground for the next year's

36

crop and was a herald of winter. Their appearance in the fall also coincides with the celebration of Halloween, when the dead are said to be able to revisit Earth, in many ways paralleling the myths of harvest and renewal.

There is another story that stresses the seasonal aspect of these stars. The Onondaga Indians of New York tell about some children who danced in autumn. An old man warned them not to, but they ignored him when he said they would starve. They were not able to find food, but continued their dancing. They became lighter and lighter and eventually floated into the heavens. These children became the Pleiades and the story reflects their rising and setting. The stars are higher when the food is scarce during the winter, their rising and setting were important signals related to the planting, harvesting, and storing of food.

The Bunjelling tribe of Australian aborigines tells of seven sisters, all intelligent and endowed with secret knowledge. A member of the tribe, Karambil, fell in love with one of the sisters, and carried her off, thus violating tribal taboos in what amounted to incest. The other six sisters objected and went off to find Winter and get his help. They sent back snow, icicles, frost, and dreadful storms. Karambil had to give in and return the sister. Only then did her sisters allow spring and summer to return. This coincides with the stars' disappearance at the beginning of the Australian winter in April and reappearance in summer in October. There are clear parallels with the Greek story of Hades carrying off Persephone, and her

mother Demeter's withholding of crops. In ancient Greece as in Australia, the threat of hunger was an excellent form of blackmail.

Many Europeans, including Hungarians, Lithuanians, Estonians, and Finns, call the Pleiades "the sieve." This is probably because of the stars' appearance during their winter, when food is scarce, winds blow, and rain falls as though through a draughty screen. The Swedes called them *Suttjenes Rauko*, or "Fur in Frost," and were seen to cover a servant whose master had driven him out into the snow.

The Greeks relate that one of the Pleiades, Electra, withdrew her light after Troy fell: her son was Dardanus, the city's founder. She returns from time to time as a comet, her long hair streaming behind her, disheveled from grief. Another version says that one of the sisters, Merope, had the temerity to marry a mortal, Sisyphus, and for this reason her light is weak. The name Merope means "mortal," "the one who appears for a day." Most ancient accounts say that there were originally seven stars, but one disappeared, perhaps Electra, from grief, or Merope, out of shame for marrying a mortal. Another candidate for the lost Pleiad is Celaeno, who was said to have been struck by lightning. The most famous sister, Maia, who sometimes is used to personify all the stars, was the mother of Hermes.

Another story of the missing Pleiad is from the *Mahabharata*, the Hindu epic of around 500 B.C. Agni, the god of fire, developed a lust for the wives of the seven

37

Rishis, or sages, but the wives rejected him. Another woman, Svaha (a star that shines from the tip of one of the horns of Taurus) lusted for Agni, who rejected her until she assumed the shape of the wives. He felt that heaven had blessed him and they continued their lovemaking until Svaha tried to assume the shape of the faithful Arundhati, one of the wives. Svaha was not able to do this, however, because even the pseudo-Arundhati could not be unfaithful. From the other unions Svaha gave birth to a boy named Skanda (well named for the scandal that followed). The husbands divorced their wives, all except Arundhati's. The other wives became the six Pleiades, and the missing one became the star Alcor, which can be seen next to her husband for eternity because all the sages became the seven stars of the Big Dipper.

In Greek the word *pleiades* means "doves," and they have been equated with the doves that fed the infant Zeus when he was in hiding. His father, Cronos, who was told that he would be overthrown by one of his children, ate each child as it was born from Rhea. In Zeus' case Rhea tricked Cronos by giving him a stone instead of the baby, whom she hid. These doves brought him ambrosia, while the goat Amalthea gave him milk. For this, Amalthea was given a horn that never failed for food—a horn of plenty.

Another Greek myth says that Orion attacked Pleione and her daughters, but Zeus turned them into the doves that can be seen as the stars that the constellation Orion still pursues. It is said that one of the doves was crushed by the Symplegades (the clashing rocks that Jason passed through), but Zeus created another. The Pleiades are also associated with the two doves on the famous cup of Nestor that is described in Homer's *Iliad*.

THIS SIXTEENTH-CENTURY FRESCO BY GIOVANNI M. FALCONETTO DEPICTS THE DEMIGOD PAN PLAYING THE PIPES THAT BEAR HIS NAME, SURROUNDED BY THE ANIMALS OF THE ZODIAC. THEY PURSUE THE DELIGHTS OF VENUS. (PALAZZO ARCO, MANTUA)

The Chinese also see these stars as young women, "the seven sisters of industry." Some Chinese traditions see only six. The Japanese Ainu think that these are six lazy girls. The Japanese themselves call the cluster *Subaru*, and show only six (one can see these six in the emblem of the car company).

The Australian aborigines see these stars as young girls playing musical instruments for young men who dance (represented by the belt stars of Orion). The Poles called them "old women," and in Russia they were "the old wife." The Hebrews called them "tents of the daughters." In Holland these are the wife of a baker and his six daughters. This relates to the Germanic legend that tells us a mother was baking bread with her six daughters when Christ passed by and was attracted by the aroma. He asked for a loaf, but had no money to pay. The baker refused, but the wife and daughters secretly gave him some. For this they were turned into seven stars in the sky, whereas the baker was turned into a cuckoo. When he sings in the spring the stars are visible. Brazilians see them as seven brothers.

Seven is a magic number, and because there are seven stars in this constellation, many groupings of seven have been associated with it. The Greeks call these stars "the seven sages." The sayings of these sages are collected in various places; two of the most famous were engraved on the temple at Delphi, namely, "Know thyself" and "Nothing in excess." Several sets of seven poets have been named after this constellation, for instance, the seven poets called the Pleiades who flourished in the third century B.C. There was a later literary Pléiade including Charlemagne, and the Greater Pléiade in sixteenth-century France under Henri III, which was followed by the Lesser Pléiade under Louis XIII.

We also find the Pleiades of Connecticut, seven poets who commemorated the American Revolution.

Some Hindus see the main star of Taurus as the "general of the celestial armies." Others see the group of stars as a flame produced by Agni, the Vedic god of fire; this would correlate with Agni's love for the wives of the sages. To commemorate these stars, the Hindus have a Feast of Lamps, which became the Feast of Lanterns in Japan.

Then again, some simply see this group as a cluster: one old Welsh name for them means "swarm." The Hebrew *Kimah* means "heap," and several South American tribes call them "group" or "pile." In "Locksley Hall," Tennyson wrote: "Many a night I saw the Pleiads, rising thro' the mellow shade/Like a swarm of fire-flies tangled in a silver braid."

The Greek word *pleiades* is associated with the word *plein*, meaning "to sail." In ancient times ships were launched at the stars' appearance in spring, and taken out of the water at the stars' setting in winter. Doves were released at the ritual ceremony when the season of navigation began, and we have noted that the Pleiades have been seen as doves. The stars are also associated with spring. In Greenland they are seen as dogs baiting a bear, and in Wales as *Y twr tewdws*, "the close pack." The Hyades have also been seen as a hen with chickens (in France, Romania, and Italy, and also by aboriginal tribes of Africa and Borneo).

Called *Matarii i Nia* ("eyes above") and *Matarii i Raro* ("eyes below"), these stars were associated with yearly cycles in Polynesia. The locals tell a story that once there was a star so large and bright that the other stars envied it. They got together and broke it into pieces, and that is how the Pleiades were formed. There have been comparable stories related by the Mayans, the Aztecs, and North American Indians, all of whom associated these stars with the seasons.

The Greeks were said to orient their temples toward the bright stars of the Pleiades, and it has been suggested that the seven chambers of the Great Pyramid in Egypt correspond to the seven Pleiades.

The emblem of St. Luke the Evangelist is a winged ox; ancient Christians also associated the bull with Saint Andrew, and with the ox that stood in the stable when Christ was born.

The Hebrews saw this constellation as Aleph, the first letter of their alphabet, which figures a bull with horns. Taurus was also important in the cult of Mithras. The Druids, too, had a festival celebrating the bull. Many of these cults relate to the moon in its phases and the horns represent a crescent.

Ursa Major, with its big dipper, may be the best-known constellation, but by far the most literary references are made to Taurus, with its famous Hyades and Pleiades, which both initiate and close the seasons. Orion and his famous belt are also located partially in this constellation.

Taurus (April 20 to May 20) is a fixed earth sign, with Venus as the governing planet. The sign's tree is an oak or apple, its flower is a daisy, and its gem is emerald or jade. Its colors are pink and blue. Taureans are compatible with Virgos and Capricorns. Taureans are slow and steady, reliable, and they have a great sense of beauty. They are practical and loyal. They like comfortable, pleasing, and peaceful surroundings. They can be stubborn and self-indulgent. They make great bankers, but can also be great poets, musicians, and artists. Distinguished people in this sign include Johannes Brahms, Charlotte Brontë, Robert Browning, Catherine the Great, Eugène Delacroix, Albrecht Dürer, Sigmund Freud, Tony Harrison, Thomas Kinsella, Karl Marx, Bertrand Russell, William Shakespeare, Piotr Tchaikovsky, and Rudolf Valentino.

GEMINI

It was from out the rind of one apple tasted that the knowledge of good and evil as two twins cleaving together leaped forth into the world.
—John Milton, Areopagitica

Starry Gemini hang like glorious crowns Over Orion's grave low down in the west.
—Alfred, Lord Tennyson, Maud

The Sumerians saw twins in the constellation Gemini, and the Greeks followed suit, most frequently identifying its two stars with the twins Castor and Pollux. These two men were also known collectively as the Dioscuri, "sons of Zeus," although only one of the men was actually the son of Zeus, by Leda. The other was the son of Tyndareus, Leda's husband, and so they are also sometimes known as the Tyndarides. The Dioscuri were the gods of Mediterranean seafarers. Castor and Pollux signaled their presence by the flame known to later peoples as St. Elmo's Fire (a double light, possibly the stars themselves).

St. Elmo's fire, a corposant (from *corpo santo*, "holy body"), could be globular or flame-shaped and could be seen at night on the mast, or at the ends of the yardarms, particularly in stormy weather. The name St. Elmo has been traced to the Dominican Pedro Gonzalez of Astorga (1190–1246) or St. Erasmus, both patrons of sailors. According to ancient Greeks, if one light appeared, there would be a storm; if two, fair weather. In modern Greece any appearance of this fire is considered warning of a shipwreck. Only the squeals of a pig can drive it and its bad luck away. In Brittany this light is considered a ghost, and prayers are offered to it. Germanic tribes thought it was a

dead mate telling them something: good weather if the light rose, bad if it fell.

There is a story that the Greek Simonides composed a poem for a Thessalian noble, but the noble complained that there was more praise for the Dioscuri than for him; when Simonides asked for his fee, he was told to get it from the Dioscuri. During a banquet that followed, two men arrived and asked for Simonides. He left, and shortly after, the palace roof caved in, killing the stingy noble. Simonides was in this way repaid by the Dioscuri for his devotion.

Castor and his brother were also great horsemen, and have been credited with the invention of chariots. Pollux gleams more powerfully than his brother, but this is understandable since he is the immortal one of the pair. Castor was more a tamer of horses, and Pollux was predominantly a boxer. He defeated the brute Amycus, who ruled the Bebryces, a people visited by the Argonauts during the quest for the golden fleece. The Olympic games were celebrated under the auspices of the twins.

Castor and Pollux also protected cities, and sided with Sparta (their mother and sisters were Spartans) at the battle of Aegospotami. They even fought on the side of Rome against the Etruscans, who wanted to restore the proud king Tarquin.

Idas and Lynceus (with unerring sight) fought with their cousins Castor and Pollux over women and cattle. When Castor and

OPPOSITE: *Rape of Leukippos' Daughters*, by Peter Paul Rubens (1577–1640). Castor and Pollux, often identified as the two brothers in Gemini, carried off Hilaera and Phoebe, daughters of the king of Messenia. In the painting you can see Cupid (or Eros) cheering the abductors on. This story is told by Theocritus in his twenty-second Idyll. (Alte Pinakothek, Munich) ABOVE: This amphora by Exekias (sixth century B.C.) shows the parting of the Dioscuri, Castor and Pollux. (Museo Gregoriano Etrusco, Vatican)

Pollux hid in a tree, Lynceus spied them out and speared Castor. Both Idas and Lynceus were killed by Pollux, who grieved so much for his brother that he shared his immortality with him so that they could live on alternating days.

Another famous pair who can be considered to be represented by this constellation are Zethus and Amphion, sons of Antiope, the daughter of the king of Thebes, and Zeus, who took the shape of a satyr (a half-goat, half-man sporting a gigantic phallus) to seduce her. Antiope's uncle Lycus forced her to expose the infants to the elements so that they would die, but shepherds saved them. Lycus then proceeded to rule the kingdom that ought to have belonged to Antiope's sons.

The two boys were different from each other. Amphion was an artist, and enjoyed playing the lyre and composing poetry. Zethus was more practical: he was strong and took care of the cattle. He criticized his brother for not doing "real work," as he did. Meanwhile, Antiope was mal-treated by her uncle Lycus, who was married to the cruel Dirce. By chance, Antiope discovered her sons and they rescued her. Dirce was torn apart by a bull, and Lycus was also killed. The kingdom of Thebes returned to the rightful heirs, and Amphion and Zethus built its walls. The stones moved to the sound of Amphion's lyre, and Zethus put them in place. Art and technology cooperated ideally in the construction of Thebes' walls.

43

Other famous Greek characters associated with these stars are Apollo and Heracles, Triptolemus and Iasion, and Theseus and Pirithous, who together carried off Helen and also attempted to carry off Persephone, bride of Hades. In the latter case they were apprehended and seated on magic thrones from which they could not rise; Heracles eventually set Theseus free, tearing his body from the throne. Pirithous, however, is still stuck firmly to his infernal seat.

The two stars of Gemini have given rise to various interpretations by world cultures. The Eskimos say that they are posts from an igloo, whereas the Arabs call them two peacocks, two gazelles, or two sprouting plants. Some of the stars form part of the Great Lion (paw) in the Arabic tradition. The Indians *Punarvarsu*, or "the two good ones," or sometimes the *Ashwins*, or "two

ABOVE, LEFT: THIS STATUE IN ROME DEPICTS ROMULUS AND REMUS, THE FOUNDERS OF THE CITY, SUCKLED BY A SHE-WOLF. **ABOVE, RIGHT:** THIS SEVENTEENTH-CENTURY CHINESE PAINTING SHOWS PEOPLE OF MIXED AGES CONTEMPLATING THE YIN-YANG, THE MALE-FEMALE DUALITY THAT UNDERLIES ALL REALITY. THIS PAIRING IS ALSO SYMBOLIZED BY GEMINI. **OPPOSITE:** THESE DEPICTIONS OF ADAM AND EVE (1507) ARE BY ALBRECHT DÜRER. (MUSEO DEL PRADO, MADRID)

horsemen." Christians saw two angels, or the twin sons of Rebecca, Jacob and Esau; David and Jonathan are also seen there, and sometimes Adam and Eve. Some Italians see this constellation as a pile of bricks and associate it with Romulus and Remus, who built Rome. This interpretation may relate to the Amphion and Zethus legend, since they built Thebes. The Hebrews identified Gemini with the tribe of Benjamin.

The Chinese include these stars in the constellation of the Ape. Later they were called *Yin* and *Yang*, or the two principles of male and female. One group of the stars was *Ta Tsun*, or "the great wine jar," and another a battle axe. One group

44

45

was "the seven feudal princes of China," and yet another, *Tseih Tsing*, "piled-up fuel." The Chinese interpretations range, as they usually do, from the exalted to the mundane.

Australian aborigines see the famous pair as young men engaged in a yearly hunt. African Bushmen think they are young women, wives of their great antelope.

The Zulus call this constellation the "Playful Twins," Masilo and Masilonyana. These twins were not popular at first in their peaceful tribe because of their savage games. They made all kinds of weapons and loved to play at war; they also excelled at sports, swimming, running, wrestling, jumping, and in general beating all the other boys in the village in athletic contests. They impressed and delighted the girls, to the

BELOW, LEFT: THIS IS A DETAIL FROM THE PYRAMID OF AMENEMHAT III AT DAHSHUR WITH HIEROGLYPHS THAT INCLUDE THE EYE OF HORUS. THE EGYPTIANS SAW HORUS IN GEMINI. HIS EYE IS A SYMBOL OF GOOD LUCK. (EGYPTIAN MUSEUM, CAIRO) BELOW, RIGHT: THIS DETAIL FROM *THE BOOK OF THE DEAD* IS FROM THE HERUBEN PAPYRUS, 21ST DYNASTY, AND SHOWS THE COBRA URAEUS, THE EYE OF HORUS, AND OTHER HIEROGLYPHS. (EGYPTIAN MUSEUM, CAIRO)

dismay of the ones who had been defeated. The king said to the boys' father that he had better advise his sons to stop these aggressive games because they were a bad example for the other children. Masilo and Masilonyana stopped such pursuits during the day, but continued at night.

One day the kingdom was attacked by a fierce animal and the king asked the boys' father if his sons would hunt down this monster and kill it. They were hot on the trail of the animal, but Masilonyana stopped to go into the bushes to urinate. The monster saw him and pierced him with a horn that it shot from its head. Another horn instantly grew again in its place. Resembling a huge goat, the monster announced that it was called Mbutiyama Tiku,

"The Death of Thousands." He tried to shoot Masilo, who deflected the horn with his shield. Masilonyana shot the beast in its eye, and it bellowed in anger and anguish. Now it grew horns with poison on the ends. The twins finally killed the beast, but they were mortally wounded doing it. The Sun God was grateful and healed them; he also granted them their wish to be joined at the shoulders so that they could be one and always fight at each other's side. When they died they were rewarded by the Earth Mother, who put them in the sky so that they could benefit mankind forever. They are also a symbol of brotherly love, unity, and devotion, and their story resembles that of Castor and Pollux.

The Zulus say that people born under this sign are very emotional and sometimes indecisive. They can give their heart to several people. They are highly creative and make fine friends. If they get angry with you, they will soon make peace. They are sensitive and can be spiritual leaders.

The ancient Egyptians saw in these stars the god Horus, who had the sun and the moon as his two eyes. Once in a battle with Set, one of Horus' eyes was torn out, but Horus was able to find it again. This is the sacred eye that can be used in numerous inscriptions and used in amulets for good fortune.

THIS CALENDAR (1416) FROM *LES TRÈS RICHES HEURES DU DUC DE BERRY*, PERHAPS THE MOST FAMOUS ILLUMINATED MANUSCRIPT, WAS ILLUSTRATED BY THE LIMBOURG BROTHERS AND SHOWS JUNE, WITH GEMINI PASSING INTO CANCER; IN THE BACKGROUND IS SAINTE-CHAPELLE AND PARIS. THESE CALENDARS SHOW HOW THE CONSTELLATIONS, SPECIFICALLY THOSE OF THE ZODIAC, WERE TIED TO SEASONAL ACTIVITIES. (MUSÉE CONDÉ, CHANTILLY)

The expression "by Jiminy" arose from swearing by the constellation Gemini. Jiminy Cricket from Disney's *Pinocchio* derives his name from this constellation, and, like the Dioscuri, is a beneficent creature.

This constellation has entered our minds and cosmic lore as a famous pair, signifying the dualities of life, such as night and day, and life and death.

Gemini (May 21 to June 21) is a mutable air sign governed by Mercury. Its plant is a palm tree, its flower lilies of the valley, and its gems jade and beryl. The colors of Gemini are yellow and blue. Geminis get along well with Libra, Capricorn, and Aquarius. People born under this sign are witty and intelligent, weigh different opinions, and enjoy change. They are talkative, sociable, energetic, and spontaneous and often have a gift for writing. Those born under Gemini bring a childlike verve to whatever they undertake, and they are very entertaining. Charm is their forte. Not surprisingly, Geminis can be good writers, salespeople, entertainers, philosophers, and teachers. Distinguished people in this sign are Alexander Cockburn, Isadora Duncan, Athol Fugard, Paul Gauguin, Thomas Hardy, Jean-Paul Sartre, Socrates, Richard Strauss, Queen Victoria, Diego Velázquez, and Richard Wagner.

47

Καρκίνος

CANCER

"I was born under Cancer, and for that reason stand on many feet, and possess much on the sea and on land, because the crab is suited to each."

—Trimalchio,
in Petronius' Satyricon

Cancer is associated with Heracles because at one point in his adventures a crab was sent by Hera to help the Hydra attack him. For its services, Hera rewarded it with stellar immortality.

The Zulus say people born under this sign are prone to sickness and must take care of themselves. They are also said to be devious. They are dreamers and poets, and are also very lucky. One myth tells of an old crab called Inkalankala. He had a young son, who walked sideways. One day his father complained, asking him why he walked sideways and not straightforward as he should. The son was puzzled and asked his father to look at the prints that he himself left in the sand: the son was walking just like his father. The Zulus have a saying that those who walk sideways have sons who also walk sideways. The myth can be likened to Aesop's fable that tells us about people who carry other people's faults in a pack in front and their own on their back: that is, it's easy to see someone else's failings.

The constellation Cancer is also depicted, first by some Roman writers and later by Bartschius and Lubienitzki in the seventeenth century, as a lobster. Other Roman writers, Ovid and Propertius, saw it as an octopus. The Mesopotamians saw the constellation as a turtle and the Egyptians saw it as the sacred beetle, *Scarabaeus*, the dung

ABOVE: This detail from *The Book of the Dead* is from the Papyrus of Anhai; it shows the solar boat, with seven of the eight Gods, the sacred beetle (a symbol of life), and the solar disk. The Egyptians saw the scarab in Cancer.

LEFT: This miniature of Cancer is from a sixteenth-century Turkish astrological treatise. Visible are the crab and the moon that governs it. (Bibliothèque Nationale, Paris)

beetle that pushes a ball of excrement it has collected into a sort of nest into which it lay its eggs. It's young thus find themselves born into a feast. Observing this, ancient people thought that the young were born spontaneously, so the beetle was associated with immortal life. This is also the beetle that, in a comic vein, took Trygaeus, in Aristophanes' *Peace*, up to heaven (just as Bellerophon was carried by Pegasus). Given the veneration of the Egyptians for this beetle—their scarab—with its close ties to immortality, it makes a good mount for those trying to reach heaven.

In both Peru and India this constellation is associated with a sacred flower. In India it was a marker for the sixth lunar station, called *Pushya*, "flower," and was depicted as a moon on the head of an arrow; the constellation was also considered the home of Brihaspati, the teacher of the gods. Another name for it in Sanskrit was *Sidhaya*, "prosperous." The Arabs see this as the mouth and muzzle of the gigantic constellation Lion, and also, like the Greeks, as two asses. The Chinese see *Kut*, the "cloud-like," formed from some of these stars, or *Kwei*, "specter." Other Chinese names for this constellation are "quail's head," "phoenix," and "red bird." Along with the constellations Leo and Virgo it denotes the home of the red, or southern, emperor.

Christians see the constellation of Cancer as the "breastplate of righteousness" and two of its stars as the "manger of the Infant Jesus." Julius Schiller dubbed it St. John the Evangelist. The Hebrews linked it with the tribe of Reuben.

The Greeks see here the two asses that helped the gods in their battle against the giants by frightening them with their braying, a strange sound the giants had never heard before. The asses were rewarded by being placed in the heavens and given a manger between them so they would

St. John the Evangelist (identified by Schiller with two stars of the constellation Cancer) appears in the right panel of an altarpiece by Hans Memling (c.1440–1494). The other two panels show (left) the decapitation of St. John the Baptist and, in the center, the Virgin and Child with saints. (Memling Museum, Bruges)

never lack for food; the nebula Praesepia is observed there, and the stars are called Praesepe, or "manger." (To the Chinese, it is known as *Tseih She Ke*, or "exhalation of piled-up corpses.")

There are other Greek tales that involve an ass. One story was about a competition between Dionysus and Ares, who were trying to reconcile Hephaestus with his mother, Hera. Ares, the god of war, went to fetch Hephaestus using his usual violence, but Hephaestus, the craftsman of the gods, was able to overcome Ares by designing superior weapons. Dionysus then said he would try. He got Hephaestus so drunk that he was easily able to lead the drunken blacksmith to Olympus; the two gods rode on asses, and the humble creatures were promoted to the heavens for their assistance.

In another tale, Hera drove Dionysus mad. Dionysus was the son of Zeus by Semele, and Hera hated him as much as she did Heracles, the son of Alkmene, another of Zeus's mortal lovers. Dionysus was told he would be cured if he consulted the oracle at Dodona, sacred to Zeus. Only an ass was able to help him cross an impossible swamp. Dionysus rewarded the ass by giving him human speech. This enabled the ass to quar-

TRIUMPH OF BACCHUS AND ARIADNE, BY AGOSTINO CARRACCI; BACCHUS, OR DIONYSUS, IS ONE OF THE GODS ASSOCIATED WITH CANCER. (FARNESE PALACE, ROME)

rel with Priapus, son of Dionysus and Aphrodite, over the relative size of their sexual members. The ass lost (fighting with gods usually being a bad idea) and was about to be cruelly slaughtered when Dionysus rescued him by substituting another ass for the slaughter. Both asses were rewarded by being placed in the heavens. They lend their names to two stars, *Asellus Borealis*, "Ass of the North," and *Asellus Australis*, "Ass of the South." The Roman writer Pliny the Elder tells us that the influence of these stars was maleficent, bringing death; when they appeared murky, rain and winds were sure to come.

Cancer is at the farthest northern point in the sky that the sun reaches. According to Chaldaean and Platonist philosophy, Cancer is regarded as a conduit through which souls pass into terrestrial life, and Capricorn was the route through which souls return to the heavens. Cancer and Capricorn give their names to the two tropics. A Chaldean priest said Earth would perish by flood when the planets joined in Cancer, and by fire when they all joined in Capricorn. The first has already happened, in June 1895, but we are still here—perhaps a god intervened on our behalf.

The constellation Cancer (June 22 to July 22) is often associated with the color red and with slow-moving animals. Cancer is a cardinal sign of water, and the moon is its "planet." Its plant is a cactus, appropriate for an animal with claws, and its colors are green, violet, and white. Its flower is jasmine. Its gem is moonstone, which is fitting for a sign governed by the moon, and Cancers are also called Moonchildren. The signs most compatible with Cancer are Scorpio and Pisces. People born under this sign are said to be creative, sensitive, cautious, and imaginative. They can be quite protective, and make good friends. Tenacity, symbolized by the crab's claws, is their virtue, and they have a tendency to offer warm support to others in need. Due to their caring, considerate natures, Cancers make wonderful nurses and doctors, and usually thrive on the domestic aspects of

52

THE NATIVITY, BY BERNADINO LUINI (C.1475–C.1532). TWO OF THE STARS IN CANCER ARE SOMETIMES REFERRED TO AS "THE MANGER OF THE INFANT JESUS."

life. Distinguished people born under this sign are Julius Caesar, Marc Chagall, Franz Kafka, Gustav Mahler, George Orwell, Marcel Proust, Rembrandt van Rijn, Jean-Jacques Rousseau, and George Sand.

Leo

Lucina, favor the birth of this child
who will make the iron age
cease, and allow a golden race to
rise throughout the world....
The goats, udders leaking milk, will
of their own accord return
home, and the rich flocks will not
fear the great lions.
—Virgil, Eclogues

The wolf also shall dwell with the
lamb, and the leopard shall
lie down with the kid; and the calf
and the young lion and the
fatling together; and a little child
shall lead them.
—Isaiah

Rise like Lions after slumber
In unvanquishable number—
Shake your chains to earth like dew
Which in sleep had fallen on you—
Ye are many—and they are few.
—Percy Bysshe Shelley,
The Mask of Anarchy

There are no oaths that can be
believed between lions and
men, nor are wolves and sheep of
like mind.
—Homer, Iliad

The wicked flee when no man pur-
sueth: but the righteous are
bold as a lion.
—Proverbs

And there the lion's ruddy eyes
Shall flow with tears of gold,
And pitying the tender cries,
And walking round the fold,
Saying: "Wrath by his meekness,
And by his health, sickness,
Is driven away
From our immortal day...."

"For washed in life's river,
My bright mane forever
Shall shine like the gold
As I guard o'er the fold."
—William Blake, Night

There is an Egyptian myth that the sun was in Leo and the moon in Cancer when the universe was created. In this constellation the Greeks saw the Nemean lion slain by Heracles. Pliny saw some of its stars as a separate constellation, "The Sickle." The Egyptians also saw a knife here. This constellation is easily recognized by its bright blue-white star, Regulus, which indicates the handle of the sickle.

Like other animals of the veldt, lions would flock to the Nile to bathe in its waters and escape the heat and drought of summer. Noticing the lions in particular, Egyptians associated the lion with the sun and the intense seasonal heat.

The Egyptian solar disc was depicted as flanked by lions. The sun in this constellation also signaled flooding in Egypt; significantly, lions were represented on the irrigation gates of the Nile. Quite possibly as a result, throughout Greece and the former Greek colonies there are many fountains with lions' heads gushing water (for instance, in Athens, Ephesus, Olympia, and Agrigento).

Dionysus often appeared in the form of a lion, and he, like Heracles, often sported a lion's skin. The lion symbolizes power, and the sun was considered the most powerful body in the heavens, so it is apt that both god and hero are associated with both the lion and the sun. The Sumerian

hero Gilgamesh was frequently shown carrying a club in one hand and a lion in the other, sharing both club and lion as power symbols with Heracles. These latter two are solar heroes, powerful, yet they came to horrible ends—Gilgamesh from leprosy and Heracles from the poisoned cloak of Nessus. These heroes were also monsters at various points in their lives, so they are good symbols for the sun, which has positive and negative aspects: in moderation the sun makes the crops grow and thrive, but in excess it can burn and destroy. The myth of Phaëthon symbolizes this dual power of the sun.

Lions are indigenous to Africa, where the Zulus say people born under this sign often become famous. They like to travel and tend to marry more than one person. They are basically lonely people, but can find friends when they need them. The African story of this constellation tells of a great flood, similar to the biblical tale of Noah and his Ark and the Greek myth of Deucalion and Pyrrha. The gods warned Grandfather Teye that a flood was coming that would overwhelm the world, and that he should build a raft and put all the humans and animals on it (clearly he had to build an enormous raft). Grandfather Teye was most persuasive and everyone came except a stubborn old lion called Mbube. Mbube said that he wanted Grandfather Teye to come and tell him only after the rains started, since he himself had grave doubts about any flood coming at all. The flood came, and the raft floated away, leaving Mbube to drown. Mbube was sorry and his pitiful cries and apologies were heard by the Sun God, who took pity on him and turned him into a constellation called "the lion left behind."

Some ancient Mediterranean astrologers claimed that the Sphinx, which has the

55

head of a woman and the body of a lion, is a composite of Leo and Virgo—the constellation that follows Leo in the zodiac. The Babylonians, Persians, Turks, Syrians, and Hebrews all saw this constellation as a lion. It was the tribal sign of Judah. It is also represented on ancient Ninevite seals in conflict with a bull, representing the victory of light over darkness. The constellation may also figure in the Mesopotamian griffin—composed of a bull, lion, scorpion, and eagle—and the Chimera, which is a fire-breathing lion and goat, and is sometimes combined with a serpent. These composites may have had astronomical significance.

ABOVE, LEFT: THIS SUMERIAN WINGED SPHINX OF IVORY AND GOLD DATES FROM THE EIGHTH OR SEVENTH CENTURY B.C. (IRAQ MUSEUM, BAGHDAD)

ABOVE, RIGHT: THIS NINTH-CENTURY B.C. ASSYRIAN RELIEF FROM THE PALACE OF ASHURNASIRPAL II AT NIMRUD DEPICTS A GRIFFIN-DEMON TENDING A SACRED TREE. (LOUVRE, PARIS)

The emblem of St. Mark the Evangelist is a lion, and some early Christians saw the apostle John in this sign. Others saw the figure of Doubting Thomas, while still others saw one of Daniel's lions.

The lion has often figured in heraldry and was so used in the crest of England. It also was used on Anglo-Norman shields in the twelfth century. Leo was occasionally represented in antiquity as standing over a snake, so it is fitting that this constellation is next to the constellation Hydra. Heavenly Leo, associated with the sun, defeats the chthonic snake, again representing the triumph of light over darkness.

In the Chinese zodiac, the horse was made up of Leo's stars. Leo also formed part of a yellow dragon, besides another of the "heavenly chariots."

The Romans called one of this constellation's bright stars Regulus, meaning "little king." It was considered a ruler of the heavens by many cultures: it was called "king" in Babylonia, "the mighty" in India, and "the great" in Persia. In Persia it is a leader of the Four Royal Stars, or Four Guardians of Heaven. The Chinese call this star *Niau*, "the bird," and with others adjacent, "the great star in *Heen Yuen*." Some other stars in this constellation are called *Woo Ti Tso*, or "the seat of the five emperors," which are surrounded by stellar followers.

On a Sumerian cup dating from 3000 B.C. is the image of a lion consuming a bull. The bull has a star between its horns, so we may take the triumph of the lion as the victory of the constellation Leo over the constellation Taurus. There may have been a fourth constellation to mark the winter solstice, composed of stars from Capricorn and Aquarius and known as the Ibex. The succes-

THE SUN IS SHOWN IN LEO, THE SIGN IT RULES, IN THIS SEVENTEENTH- OR EIGHTEENTH-CENTURY INDIAN MINIATURE ON PAPER, POSSIBLY FROM THE SCHOOL OF DELHI. (PIERPONT MORGAN LIBRARY, NEW YORK CITY)

sion of the seasons can be represented as the victory of one animal over another.

The Assyrian constellation Asad is a gigantic lion that stretches over many constellations. Some of the stars were designated the front of the lion and its mane, and another is known as "He who varies," which may refer to the weather during the summer months.

Leo (July 23 to August 22) is a fixed fire sign, governed by the sun. Its tree is the pine tree, its flower is the marigold, and its gem is the ruby. Its color is orange. Signs compatible with Leo are Gemini and Sagittarius. As a sign, it is associated with power and wealth. Leos are natural leaders, though they are sometimes proud and jealous. They are also fond of children, and thus make good parents. They are dramatic, enthusiastic, good at organizing, and very generous. Those born under this sign make good business people, politicians, professors, excellent public speakers, and entertainers. Some well-known Leos are Emily Brontë, Claude Debussy, Carl Jung, Guy de Maupassant, Benito Mussolini, Napoleon, George Bernard Shaw, Percy Bysshe Shelley, and Mae West.

Κόρη

VIRGO

Now does the virgin return, and the
reign of Saturn,
now a new race descends from the
lofty heavens.
　　　　—Virgil, Eclogues

This is the month, and this the
happy morn
Wherein the son of heaven's eternal
king,
Of wedded maid, and virgin mother
born,
Our great redemption from above
did bring.
　　—John Milton, "On the Morning
of Christ's Nativity"

Where the Youth pined away with
desire,
And the pale Virgin shrouded in
snow,
Arise from their graves and aspire
Where my Sun-flower wishes to
go.
　　　　　—William Blake,
　　　　　"Ah, Sun-flower"

Every harlot was a virgin once.
　　—William Blake, For the Sexes:
The Gates of Paradise

58

Virgo is the only woman in the zodiac: the other three human signs are all male. Thus, she combines all the traditional aspects of the female: the maiden, the matron, and the old woman.

Located next to her father, Icarius, or Boötes, the constellation Virgo is identified with Erigone, whose story is recounted by Eratosthenes of Cyrene, a learned scholar at the library of Alexandria, which was famous in antiquity. Eratosthenes tells the story of how Erigone's father was visited by the god Dionysus, who gave

OPPOSITE:

PROSERPINA, BY DANTE GABRIEL ROSSETTI (1828–1882). THIS DAUGHTER OF CERES (DEMETER IN THE GREEK), WHO WAS CARRIED OFF BY PLUTO (OR HADES), MAY BE THE MAIDEN THAT IS REPRESENTED BY VIRGO. (TATE GALLERY, LONDON)

him in return for his generous hospitality the vine from which wine is made. A goat was sacrificed to provide food for the feast and the skin was used for a wine flask. Erigone was also given the gift of a child by Dionysus, called Staphylus, whose name means "grape" in Greek. Eratosthenes links this myth with the birth of tragedy (the word "tragedy" etymologically stems from the Greek for "goat-song"), and Dionysus is the god of tragedy. Eratosthenes sees in this constellation a group of celebrants dancing around a wine flask made from goatskin; historians believe that ritual celebrants enacted the first dramas as dances in honor of the god.

Virgo the maiden is associated with Demeter, or her daughter, Persephone. Yet others associate Virgo with the Babylonian Ishtar, or the Egyptian Isis, or the Syrian Atargatis. She is a source of fertility and symbol of the mature harvest and is often shown holding an ear of sprouting grain—the brightest star in this constellation is Spica, which means "ear of grain." The Sumerians called this star *Ab-sin*, which was considered the goddess Shala's ear of grain. E.C. Krupp, in *Beyond the Blue Horizon: Myths and Legends of the Sun, Moon, Stars, and Planets*, argues that Shala meant "woman" and in one inscription is called "The Lady of the Field." He points out that *Ab-sin* means "furrow": "A furrow is the field's vulva. Before it is seeded, the furrow is a virgin; after seeding, it bears new life. It is said in the *Odyssey*...that Demeter coupled in love with Iasion, lying in the plowed furrow of fallow land. The star [Spica] was probably the celestial signal for ploughing or planting in the Sumerian era." This would explain the many depictions of Virgo the maiden holding ripe grain and relate to the cycle of planting and harvesting that is associated with so many stars and constellations.

Demeter's daughter, Persephone, was kidnaped by Hades while she was gathering flowers in Sicily. Grief-stricken, Demeter refused to allow grain to grow; people starved and became too weak to sacrifice to the gods. Finally Demeter's pleas were heard, and she was allowed to be with her daughter for nine months of the year, during which time the world flourished. The other three months of the year (winter) Persephone spends in dark Hades, and at this time the grain is dormant. The star *Spica* is the grain she carries.

59

The Aztecs also called this constellation Mother Earth, or the Magical Mother. "Mother" is associated with food, hence grain. In the temperate zones of the northern hemisphere, harvest-time takes place when the sun is in Virgo. Perhaps this explains why this constellation has similar designations throughout the world, since the star pattern is hardly obvious.

The constellation Virgo may also be identified with the original mother goddess that ruled the Mediterranean in various guises in Minoan Greek, Syrian, Phoenician, Babylonian, and Egyptian traditions, among other cultures, as described by Robert Graves in *The White Goddess*. To single out the Greek tradition, she was ruler of the heavens as goddess of the moon (Artemis or *kore*, "the virgin"), of the earth (Demeter), and of the underworld (Hecate). One sees in these guises the unripe grain, the mature grain, and the harvested grain. One of her later transformations was into the Virgin Mary, who in giving birth to Jesus was the origin of man's redemption, allowing the rebirth of his soul.

As Ishtar, she mourns the loss of her lover Tammuz, just as Aphrodite did Adonis. Both lovers were gored by boars. Ishtar went to the underworld to retrieve her beloved, and while she was held there the world grew barren. Ea (Capricorn), a god of water, ordered Ereshkigal, the queen of the underworld, to release both

BELOW: THIS SYRO-PHOENICIAN SCULPTURE OF ISHTAR BETWEEN TWO SPHINXES IS OF CARVED HORN. (NATIONAL MUSEUM, DAMASCUS)

OPPOSITE: *WHEAT HARVEST*, BY CLAUDE GOUFFIER, IS FROM A SIXTEENTH-CENTURY BOOK OF HOURS AND DEPICTS A TYPICAL LATE-SUMMER SCENE. (BIBLIOTHÈQUE DE L'ECOUEN, FRANCE)

Tammuz and Ishtar so that the earth could flourish again. This tale clearly parallels the myth of Demeter.

The year is symbolized by these myths with the springtime of love, the summer that leads to death, and the harvest, and then the winter during which the seeds lie dormant. Spring comes again, with love and rebirth. As a sign of this renewal, both Aphrodite (Venus, goddess of love) and Ishtar are identified with the morning (Phosphorus) and evening stars (Hesperus, actually the planet Venus). Venus blesses the night with promise of love, then ushers in the day, in charge of the cycle of rebirth. Ishtar was identified with the Hebrew Astoreth mentioned in the *Book of Kings*, and links can be traced between Aphrodite, Hathor, and the Syrian Astarte, or even Esther.

Various African peoples were also aware of the sexual aspect of this sign. They thought that people born under this sign were exquisite lovers and great organizers, and like the moon that governs them, subject to bright and dark phases. The myth associated with this constellation is a cautionary tale, concluding that it is dangerous to give a woman too much power; her sexuality should be power enough. The Tswana- and Sotho-speaking tribes named this star Gadi, "the woman," or Muretsama, "the bride." These were

her generic names, but her particular name was Nanana, and she was the daughter of the Moon God; her mother was the chief of a tribe of frogs who could only say, "Nanana, nanana."

Nanana was young, beautiful, and ambitious. She wanted to rule the gods and to steal the golden branch of power from God the Father. She cast a spell on him and he became very sick. Earth Mother cast the sacred bones and learned that Nanana was to blame for God the Father's illness and would only release him if she could have the golden branch. She was given it reluctantly, and God the Father recovered. But every time Nanana cast a spell with the branch it withered a bit, so that finally all she had was a wilted, impotent stick. She threw it in anger at God the Father, who picked it up; it was immediately

ABOVE: *JUSTICE*, BY DOMENICO BECCAFUMI (1486–1551). VIRGO IS SOMETIMES, LIKE LIBRA, IDENTIFIED WITH THE CONCEPT OF JUSTICE. SHE MAY REPRESENT DIKE, THE GODDESS OF JUSTICE WHO ABANDONED THE WORLD AS UNWORTHY OF HER PRESENCE. (PALAZZO PUBBLICO, SIENA)

restored to its original golden potency. (It could be used to illustrate Freud's fantasy that women have penis envy. It is obvious that the myth was made up by a man, concerned about keeping women "in their place." Anyway, if there is any envy of man, it is for the power he assumes.)

In India, Virgo is called *Kanya*, "the maiden," mother of Krishna. Sinhalese see it as "woman in the ship," carrying a stalk of wheat. Persians see it as *Khosha*, "the ear of wheat."

To the Arabs this constellation was part of the gigantic Lion they saw in this area of the heavens. Later, with more travel between cultures, they also saw it as a maiden—not in human shape but only as the simple wheat stalk. Arabs called its stars "the kennel corner of the barking dogs," or even just "the dogs."

The Turcomans called this constellation *Dufhiza Pakhiza*, "the pure maiden," and the Chinese called it *She Sang Neu*, "the frigid maiden." Earlier Chinese interpretations cast the constellation as a snake or the tail of a quail, a pheasant, or a phoenix. These early Chinese observers saw Spica as *Kio*, "the torn," and it was considered a star of spring. Another star was called *Sheu Sing*, or "the star of old age."

By the Greeks, Virgo is also seen as Justice, or Dike, the goddess who left the world when it became so wicked that humankind no longer merited her presence. Aratus in the *Phaenomena* relates that she used to mix freely with men of the Golden Race. She still advised those of the Silver Race, but when the brutal Bronze Race appeared with its endless wars, she flew off to heaven and became the constellation Virgo. She

LEFT: *KRISHNA ON THE SWING* (C.1750–1760), BY GULER, SHOWS THE HINDU GOD WITH HIS MOTHER, KANYA, THE MAIDEN, WHO IS IDENTIFIED WITH THE CONSTELLATION VIRGO. (BRITISH MUSEUM, LONDON) RIGHT: THIS EGYPTIAN STATUE DEPICTS ISIS NURSING HORUS. ISIS IS ANOTHER OF THE MANY FACES OF VIRGO. (VATICAN CITY) OPPOSITE: THIS DETAIL FROM A LOVELY CELESTIAL GLOBE MADE BY JOSEPH JEROME LELANDE IN 1775 SHOWS VIRGO, THE VIRGIN. (PRIVATE COLLECTION, VIENNA)

is associated with her sisters Eunomia, or "just law," and Eirene, "peace."

Virgo is also identified with Tyche or Fortuna, the revolving wheel of fortune (fortune also has its own seasons). This constellation also represents Moirai, the three fates: Clotho, the one who spins; Lachesis, the one who deals out lots, or measures the threads of mortal life; and Atropos, the one who cannot be avoided, who cuts the thread. They are the masters of life and death.

Isis, the Egyptian lunar goddess, loses Osiris the lunar god, whose rending at the hands of the evil Set is avenged by her son Horus (the young moon). In depictions of Isis, the snake at her feet is the force of darkness that she overcomes (that is, Set, whose classical Greek counterpart is the monster Typhon). Osiris' rebirth coincides with the yearly flooding of the Nile. The constellation Virgo is also associated with the Sphinx, the female head (Virgo) on the body of a lion (Leo) at the time of the yearly flood. Others see the head as an Egyptian god (Harmachis). Isis is often represented as carrying the infant Horus, and one can see similar representations of the Virgin Mary carrying Jesus, and porla Coupe

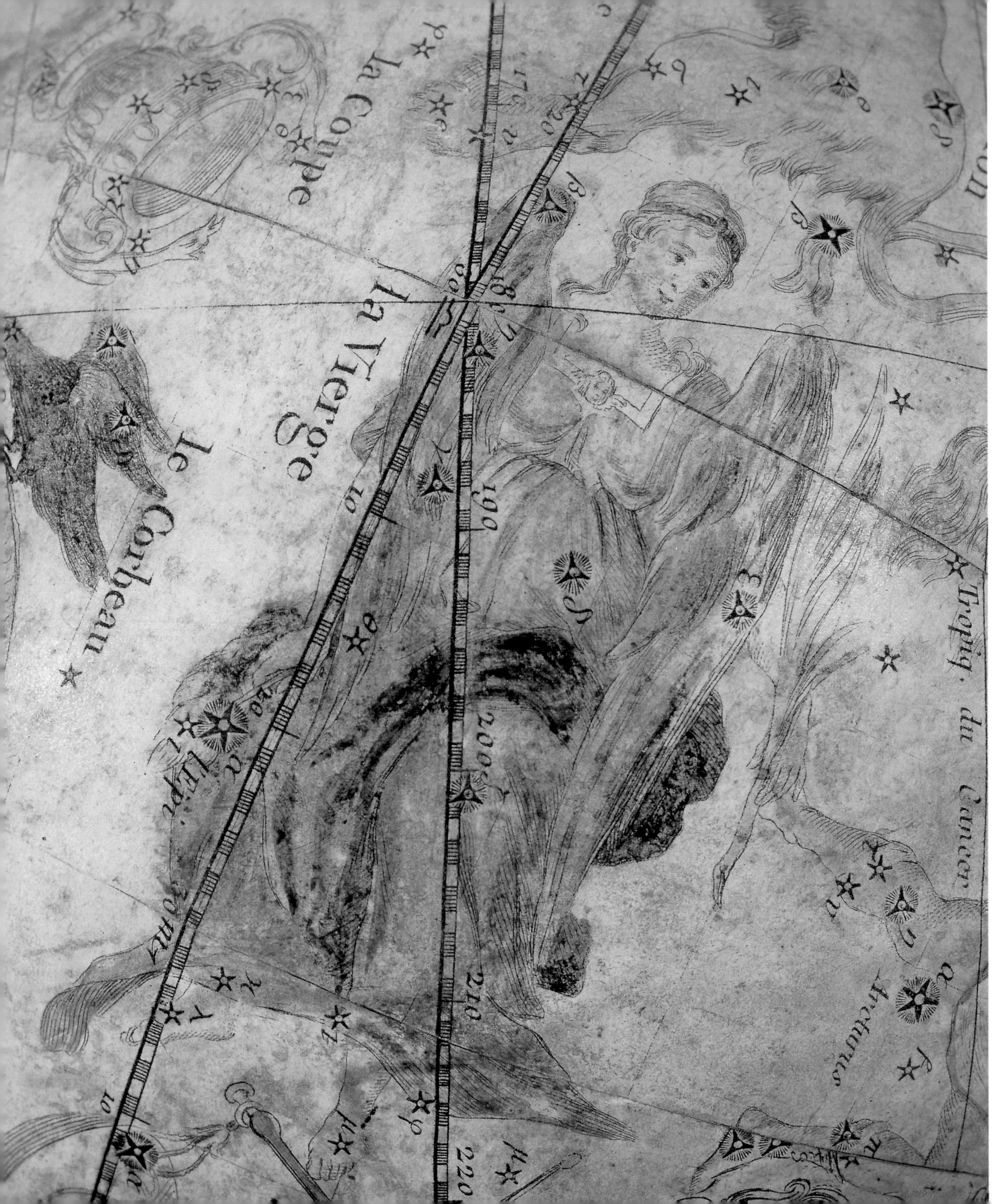

la Vierge

le Corbeau

le Corbeau

Tropiq. du Cancer

Arcturus

trayed with a moon at her feet and stars on her robe, symbols that also link her with Isis. Many symbols associated with and many attributes ascribed to the Virgin Mary have parallels among ancient fertility goddesses. For instance, both Isis and the Virgin are sometimes represented as black (in their Mediterranean manifestations).

Another Christian association of this constellation was with St. James the Less, the apostle known as "the Lord's brother." The Hebrew tribe associated with this sign is Gad. Hindus saw Spica as *Citra,* meaning "bright," and it was represented as a lamp, or a pearl.

The many associations of Virgo with a maiden and mother in western interpretations of this constellation demonstrates the woman's control over life, being able to give it, withhold it, and take it away. Although in early times the Arabs and Chinese had very different interpretations of this constellation (instead of a young maiden, they saw an old man or an animal), after communication with the West, the overriding association with femaleness in all its aspects prevailed. In some sense, perhaps, this constellation is a bright warning not to meddle with Mother Nature.

IN THE CHRISTIAN TRADITION, VIRGO REPRESENTS THE VIRGIN MARY, OR MADONNA. THIS IS A HAND-COLORED COPY OF A PAINTING BY V.M. VASNETOFF. (VLADIMIR CATHEDRAL, KIEV)

Virgo (August 23 to September 22) is a mutable earth sign; its planetary ruler is Mercury. Its plant is wheat (the sheaf that Demeter gave to Triptolemus, or the gift of grain to man) and its flower is lavender; its gem is peridot or agate (a stone that is usually green, like the flourishing earth). Its colors are green, blue, and gray-brown. Virgos are said to get along well with those born under the signs of Capricorn and Taurus. Because Virgos are notoriously orderly and precise (some might go so far as to say fussy and critical), people born under this sign tend to make good mathematicians and precise scholars. They can be very cautious— even overly so, at times. As far as occupations go, Virgos are often critics, accountants, engineers, workers in technology (particularly computers), inspectors, secretaries, doctors, nurses, editors, and teachers. Generally speaking, Virgos are good at study and service. They are also known for being extremely loyal friends. Notable people born under this sign include Queen Elizabeth I, Johann Wolfgang von Goethe, Gustav Holst, George Huxley, Cardinal Richelieu, Mother Teresa, Leo Tolstoy, and H.G. Wells.

Ζυγόν
LIBRA

Then the father [of the gods, Zeus] held up the golden scales, and on each side loaded the two fates of sorrow–bringing death [for Hector and Achilles]...the fatal day for Hector sank down.
—Homer, Iliad

Thou art weighed in the balances, and art found wanting.
—The Book of Daniel

[Imagination] reveals itself in the balance or reconciliation of opposite or discordant qualities.
—Samuel Taylor Coleridge, Biographica Literaria

Like Gemini, the constellation Libra is associated with duality, the two bowls of the scales, though it may originally have been linked with Scorpio's pincers. The Arabs give the two main stars the names "Southern and Northern Claw." The Babylonians mention a pair of scales in this area of the sky, but the early Greeks did not include a scale in their zodiac, seeing instead Scorpio's claws. It is said that after the astronomer Hipparchus (flourished around 150 B.C.), who catalogued some 850 stars, the Greeks changed the name to scales. These may be the scales held by Astraea, the virgin goddess of justice, one of the representations of Virgo.

Libra also meant a lot to the Roman Caesars and astrologers; it was included in the Julian Calendar. Julius Caesar would often represent himself on coins with scales, signifying his authority and sense of justice. Both he and Augustus were associated with this constellation.

Statues depicting Justice frequently hold a scale in one hand, blindfolded to signify her impartiality. In front of Ireland's main government building the statue of Justice holds scales, but she is not blindfolded. She also faces into the building, and her back is to Dublin proper. This has led to the rueful comment among the Irish that there was justice only for those in power—namely the British.

IVSTITIA

This constellation may also represent the scales that the Homeric Zeus used to determine man's fate. The Egyptian tradition viewed this constellation as the scales used by Osiris to weigh the dead to determine their reward in the afterlife. Most likely this scale with two pans signifies the equality of day and night at the time of the fall equinox, when the sun enters this sign. It is a time of plentitude and celebration of the harvests. This is also a time of moderation, neither the burning heat of summer on one side, represented by the hot-tempered Leo, nor the cold bite of winter on the other, represented by Sagittarius' arrows.

Christians identify this constellation with the apostle Philip, the Hebrews with the tribe Asher. The Chinese call some stars in Libra *Ti,* "the bottom," and another star *Show Sing,* "the star of longevity." Once it was "the crocodile," or "dragon," the national symbol of the country; other stars simply designate an area of China called *Se Han.* The Indians call it "a balance," but also "fire." Hebrews called it *Moznayim,* "a scale-beam." There is some evidence that early people from the Euphrates River valley saw this constellation as an altar, and then again as a lamp. Another Greek interpretation was that it was the chariot that carried off Persephone.

Libra, representing justice, is the only sign of the zodiac that is inanimate. It may be the case that early observers wanted to honor the ideal of justice; more cynically, the scales may have been placed in the heavens to point out the absence of justice on Earth.

To the Zulus the sign is named after a wise judge. They think people born under this sign are skeptics who take

OPPOSITE: *La Giustizia,* by Giulio Romano (1499–1546). Libra is often associated with justice, a concept symbolized by the scales that weigh the good against the bad. (Stanze di Raffaello, Vatican City) RIGHT: This German bronze statuette of justice, *Justitia,* dates from 1890. (Archiv für Kunst und Geschichte, Berlin)

nothing on faith; they like to investigate life to its depths. They will do anything for a friend, and also love to hunt. But once those born under Libra get what they are seeking, they go on to new quests.

The related myth concerns a king's son named Gubudela. When he was a boy he played with dolls instead of oxen, and when he grew up he liked to do women's tasks. He was a master weaver, and the beauty of his baskets so annoyed the women of the tribe that they complained to the *Sangoma,* or shaman. He brought their complaint to the Earth Mother, who summoned Gubudela and had two zombies roll him up in a rug so he could not move. When

LEFT: JACKAL-HEADED ANUBIS, GOD OF THE DEAD, LEADING THE DISEASED AND ATTENDING THE SCALES FOR RECORDING SIN. THIS IS A DETAIL FROM *THE BOOK OF THE DEAD*, FROM THE PAPYRUS OF HUNEFER. THE ASSOCIATION OF JUSTICE WITH THE SCALES IS COMMON TO COUNTLESS CULTURES AROUND THE WORLD. (BUDGE COLLECTION)

they unwrapped the rug he had become a beautiful woman. Since she knew what it was to be both man and woman, she was widely sought after as a wise judge. The people seeking her advice were to fill two baskets, and Gubudela used them to make her decisions. She lived a long and productive life and was so respected that she was put in the heavens where she still holds her two baskets and delivers wise decisions.

The classical Greek parallel is Tiresias, who spent time as both a man and a woman. He irritated Hera when she asked him who had more sexual pleasure, a man or a woman, and he answered that the pleasure was nine-tenths the woman's.

BELOW: *The Rape of Proserpina*, by LAMBERT SUSTRIS, SHOWS THE MYTH THAT EXPLAINS THE REASON FOR THE SEASONS. (UPTON HOUSE, OXFORDSHIRE)

Libra (September 23 to October 23) is a cardinal air sign governed by Venus. Its flowers are the lily and orchid, and its gem is opal. Its colors are light blue, dark blue, and pink. The most compatible signs are Aquarius and Gemini. Libras are conciliators, with a strong sense of beauty and balance. They can be poets, musicians, dramatists, or actors. They are romantic, flirtatious, idealistic, firm friends, and excellent diplomats. They are great travelers and can be good politicians or business people. Distinguished people born under this sign are Brigitte Bardot, Sarah Bernhardt, Mohandas Gandhi, Franz Lizst, Friedrich Nietzsche, Tintoretto, Gore Vidal, Virgil, Oscar Wilde, and Ralph Vaughan Williams.

SCORPIO

Look for a scorpion, my friend,
under every stone.
—Praxilla

O, full of scorpions is my mind,
dear wife!
—William Shakespeare, Macbeth

The heart of the Scorpion has set,
the tyrant in man has fled,
and all the daughters of the sea,
Nereids, Graeae,
hurry to the radiance of the rising
goddess:
whoever has never loved will love,
in the light....
—Seferis, Thrush, III

72

S corpio may represent the scorpion that plagued Orion, sent either by Apollo or Artemis. It may also commemorate the scorpion men whom Orion met when he was searching for immortality. The scorpion was said to have frightened Phaëthon as he drove his father's solar chariot, causing him to lose control of the horses, who then plunged closer to Earth and scorched many areas before finally crashing down into the river Eridanus (also represented by stars in the sky). Both Orion and Phaëthon are associated with the sun, which becomes weak at

OPPOSITE: *THE FALL OF PHAËTHON,* BY BERNADINO GALLIARI (1707–1794). THE SCORPION FRIGHTENED THE HORSES OF THE SOLAR CHARIOT, DRIVEN BY THE UNSKILLED HANDS OF PHAËTHON, CAUSING THE BEASTS TO BOLT MADLY AND OVERTURN THE CHARIOT. (GALLERIA SABAUDA, TURIN)

this time of year. The ancient Greeks considered Scorpio a threat to light because the sun diminished after the equinox.

This constellation features stars that form the shape of a scorpion, with twin pincers and a curved tail. Long ago the constellation was larger; during the time of Caesar, the claws were trimmed to create the constellation Libra. Sumerians saw a lamp or beacon between the claws. Christians saw the constellation as the apostle St. Bartholomew, or then again, as a cardinal's hat. Hebrews took it for a crowned

snake, or the emblem of the tribe of Dan. The Akkadians may have seen it as a double sword. The Persians also saw it as a scorpion.

Ancient Egyptians saw the star Antares as Isis, and others as the goddess Selkit. Both Egyptian and Greek temples were oriented towards the ancient rising and setting of this star at the time of the spring equinox.

Some Chinese observers considered this constellation part of the Azure Dragon; some also thought it was the residence or council chamber of the Emperor, with Antares in charge and the other stars representing courtiers milling about.

ABOVE, LEFT: THIS DETAIL FROM THE **S**ISTINE **C**HAPEL HIGHLIGHTS **S**T. **B**ARTHOLOMEW, ASSOCIAT-ED IN THE **C**HRISTIAN CANON WITH **S**CORPIO. (**S**ISTINE **C**HAPEL, **V**ATICAN **C**ITY) **ABOVE, RIGHT: T**HIS RELIEF FROM HER TOMB SHOWS **C**LEOPATRA AS **I**SIS, ASSOCIATED WITH THE STAR **A**NTARES IN THE CONSTELLATION **S**CORPIO.

Other Chinese called Antares "the fire star," and Antares with the stars of the scorpion's tail, "a divine temple." It also represents the hare in the Chinese zodiac. Certain stars in the grouping were seen as a "four-horse chariot of heaven," revered by horsemen. Others called these stars "the basket with handles," which was important for raising silkworms, and indicative of the season when that industry began.

Polynesians saw the curved stars of the scorpion's tail as "the fish-hook of Maui," used by the god to fish up the islands Tongareva, Hawaii, and New Zealand. Some say the

Orion in December (1969), a watercolor with pencil by Charles E. Burchfield, is a wonderful representation of the constellation Orion. Clearly visible are the three stars in the Belt of Orion. In myth, Orion was plagued by a scorpion sent by Apollo or Apollo's twin sister, Artemis. (National Museum of American Art, Washington, D.C.)

fishhook was made out of the jawbone of Maui's ancestress. (Once when Maui thought the sun was going over the heavens too fast, he caught it and beat it with this jawbone to slow it down.) The Polynesians also saw two of the stars as a little girl, Piri-ere-ua, and her small brother fleeing from abusive parents.

The scorpion, like the dragon or the serpent, is a force of darkness, even death, in the classical tradition. Just as Ophiuchus crushes the scorpion underfoot as he wrestles a serpent, so Hercules crushes the serpent Draco. In trying to overcome these wild creatures, both heroes are symbolically trying to overcome death, in much the same way as the Sumerian hero Gilgamesh. Hercules won immortality, but Orion, Ophiuchus, and Gilgamesh did not. Of course, if one way to overcome death is to be promoted to the stars, then all three heroes have achieved immortality.

The Zulus also see a scorpion in this constellation. Just as Hera rewarded her obedient crab, snake, and hundred-eyed monster Argus, so the Earth Mother of the African tradition rewarded her pet scorpion,

THIS SIXTEENTH-CENTURY TURKISH MINIATURE IS FROM AN ASTROLOGY BOOK AND SHOWS THE CONSTELLATION SCORPIO. (BIBLIOTHÈQUE NATIONALE, PARIS)

Sobatinyela. She created him so that he would be the faithful guardian of her home. Once, she was on a trip and God the Father saw a mermaid who captivated him with her beauty. He made love to her every day in his home while his wife was away, but this angered Sobatinyela so much that the scorpion stung God the Father in one of his buttocks as he was making love. It immediately swelled up and gave him terrible pain, so he looked around for the cause and found Sobatinyela, whom he crushed with one blow. Earth Mother returned home and missed her faithful guardian, so she consulted the magic bones, which told her the whole story. She found Sobatinyela's remains and put them in the heavens as a reward.

For these Africans, people born under this sign fight for causes sometimes to the death. They try to reform the world, but can have a bad temper. They are known for exacting vengeance, sometimes for imagined wrongs.

Scorpio (October 24 to November 21) is a fixed water sign, and was ruled by Mars, but some astrologers now say

76

that Pluto (discovered in 1930) rules this sign. Its flower is a water lily (beautiful on top, and rooted in mud) and its gem is alexandrite, a stone that is green in sunlight and red-violet in artificial light. Some claim topaz is Scorpio's primary gem. Both the water lily and alexandrite show the dual nature of people in this sign: a beautiful public life and a second secret life, grounded in passion and the earth. The sign's colors are red and black. Particularly compatible signs are Capricorn, Cancer, and Pisces. People born

AN ILLUSTRATION OF THE GROUPING OF STARS KNOWN AS SCORPIO, FROM AN EIGHTEENTH-CENTURY BOOK OF THE CONSTELLATIONS.

under this sign are strong, cold yet fiery (beware their temper), secretive, stubborn, passionate, imaginative, resourceful, and brilliantly intuitive. They are heroic, yet can also be vindictive. They are good in the areas of law enforcement and writing, and make passionate workers for good causes. Distinguished people born under this sign are Fyodor Dostoyevsky, John Keats, Claude Monet, Pablo Picasso, Ezra Pound, August Rodin, Edward Said, Domenico Scarlatti, Jan Vermeer, and Voltaire.

Τοξευτής SAGITTARIUS

*The cloud-centaurs were marching
towards us...they were a combination of winged horses and men.
The men (the top half) were as
large as the Colossus of Rhodes,
and the horses were larger than a
huge ship....Their leader was the
archer from the Zodiac.*
—Lucian, A True Story

*My men, like satyrs grazing on the
lawns,
Shall with their goat feet dance an
antic hay.*
—Christopher Marlowe,
Edward II

*With sounding hoofs across the
earth I fly,
A steed Thessalian with a human
face.*
—Henry Wadsworth Longfellow,
Poet's Calendar

An angel satyr walks these hills.
—Francis Kilvert,
Selections from the Diary

*Two creatures face each other, fixed
in song,
Satyr and nymph, across the dark-
ening brain.
I dream of reason and the first
grows strong,
Drunk as a whirlwind on the
sweating grain;
I dream of drunkenness and, freed
from strain,
The second murmurs like a fingered
gong;
I sink beneath the dream: his words
grow sane,
Her pupils glow with pleasure all
night long.*
—Thomas Kinsella, "Fire and Ice"

In the classical Greek tradition, the constellation Sagittarius, the Archer, is directly
associated with the hero Orion; the Sumerians identified it with Enkidu, Gilgamesh's
beloved. But the two myths are related: both
Orion and Gilgamesh attacked the heavenly
bull, reflected by the fact that, at opposite points
on the zodiac, Sagittarius is visible when Taurus
is not, and vice versa. In a sense, each constellation leads to
the death of the other, nicely paralleling the drama of the
two heroes.

OPPOSITE: *CENTAUR AND NYMPH* BY FRANZ VON STUCK (1863–1928), SHOWS AN AMOROUS CENTAUR EMBRACING A NYMPH. (GEMÄLDEGALERIE, DRESDEN)

Sagittarius is one of the four human signs,
though in the western tradition it is portrayed as
a centaur (half-man, half-horse) armed with a
bow and arrow (*sagitta,* in Latin). (Because it is
half-human, half-beast, Sagittarius is also associated with satyrs.) Some of the related myths
concern the centaur, the most famous of whom
was Chiron, the teacher of gods and heroes.
Symbolically, the centaur as a creature embodies the duality
of both Enkidu (the beast-man who acted in a civilized way)
and Gilgamesh (the civilized man who acted like a beast).

One centaur story concerns Crotos, the son of Eupheme, nurse of the Muses. Crotos invented the bow and was a skilled horseman, but most of all he applauded the performances of the Muses. In appreciation, the muses put him in the heavens in a form that related to his skills: he was part horse because of his horsemanship; he was given a bow to commemorate his archery; the tail of a satyr was added to his starry shape because he entertained the Muses as much as the satyrs did Dionysus.

In the fifth century B.C. in Greece, the Milky Way was thought to be a resting place for people's souls, which left the mortal world through the doors of Sagittarius and reentered through Gemini. (As noted earlier, Cancer and Capricorn were considered alternate routes.)

In Sumerian inscriptions the constellation is interpreted as Nergal, the archer god of war. The Indians saw it simply as a bow and arrow. The Hebrews took the bow as a tribal symbol for Ephraim and Manasseh. Christians saw Joash shooting arrows as commanded by Elisha. It has been called Ishmael, and is also linked to the tribe of Benjamin. For Christians, this constellation was sometimes interpreted as the apostle and evangelist Saint Matthew.

Some Arabs saw this constellation as ostriches returning from and going to the Milky Way to drink. One star is their keeper. There is also an "ostrich nest" star grouping nearby. Then again, these stars were sometimes interpreted as camels or cattle, or an overturned chair or a necklace. On the roof of the Temple of Hathor at Dendera in Egypt, Sagittarius is depicted wearing a crown: since Corona Australis is so near, it is easy to see it as Sagittarius' crown.

OPPOSITE, TOP: THIS RED-FIGURE ATTIC VASE PAINTING, WHICH DEPICTS A GALLOPING CENTAUR ARMED WITH A ROCK AND A TREE TRUNK, WAS MADE BY THE POTTER AND VASE-PAINTER PHINTIAS, C. 520–510 B.C. CENTAURS WERE CONSIDERED SAVAGE CREATURES, WITH A FEW NOTABLE EXCEPTIONS. (BADISCHES LANDESMUSEUM, KARLSRUHE) OPPOSITE, BOTTOM: *NYMPH AND SATYR*, PETER PAUL RUBENS (1577–1640). SAGITTARIUS IS ASSOCIATED WITH SATYRS AS WELL AS CENTAURS. SATYRS HAVE EVEN WORSE REPUTATIONS THAN CENTAURS AS (USUALLY AMOROUS) MISCHIEF-MAKERS, AS IS EVIDENT IN THIS PICTURE. (GEMÄLDEGALERIE, DRESDEN) RIGHT: *ALLEGORY OF OBEDIENCE* (C.1320), BY GIOTTO (C.1266–1337), SHOWS ST. FRANCIS MARRYING OBEDIENCE. VISIBLE IS A CENTAUR. GIVEN ITS MYTHICAL REPUTATION, THE CENTAUR IS LIKELY SYMBOLIC OF THE BASER DRIVES AND GENERAL PAGAN IMPULSES THAT ST. FRANCIS SUBDUED WHEN HE MARRIED OBEDIENCE AND DEDICATED HIMSELF TO THE SERVICE OF GOD. (CHURCH OF SAN FRANCESCO, ASSISI)

The Zulus consider people born under this sign to have good insight and be willing to help others. They are also great fighters and fine actors, and in general perform well before the public. They can sometimes be extremists. The related myth tells of Sozabile, a giant who had the head of a hare, a bow in one hand, and a hare in the other hand. Nogwaja, a trickster who was also shaped like a hare, wanted to dupe Sozabile. Nogwaja challenged Sozabile to drink a river dry, but at night he got his children to connect the river to another so that it would be impossible to drain. Sozabile got Lulwane the bat to help him; the bat was able to counter what Nogwaja had done, restoring the river to its proper place so that Sozabile won the bet. Sozabile grabbed Nogwaja and pretended to cook him, to scare him, as a lesson to be careful with his tricks. After he taught the trickster his lesson he returned to the stars.

The Chinese see the stars of Sagittarius as a sieve (and other stars as a ladle, a mouth, heels, and a temple). The general constellation was known as "the tiger," part of it comprised the Azure Dragon. Some stars were seen as "general of the wind," others as "flagstaff," and some as "the dog's country."

Sagittarius (November 22 to December 21) is a mutable fire sign ruled by Jupiter. Its flower is the bird of paradise, its tree maple, and its gem is sapphire or turquoise. The colors are shades of blue and violet. Sagittarians get along especially well with Aries and Leos. They are loyal friends who tell the truth: their words hit the mark. They are optimistic, sincere, and like adventure. They can be creative leaders, good lawyers, veterinarians, and doctors. They may burn with idealism, and are particularly good in sports or academia. Outstanding people born under this sign are Jane Austen, Ludwig van Beethoven, Hector Berlioz, William Blake, Winston Churchill, Joseph Conrad, Horace, Paul Klee, John Milton, Jean Sibelius, Henri de Toulouse-Lautrec, and Mark Twain.

THIS ILLUSTRATION SHOWS AN ANGEL PASSING IN FRONT OF THE CONSTELLATION SAGITTARIUS AS IT PURSUES SCORPIO THROUGH THE HEAVENS.

82

CAPRICORN

The gods, that mortal beauty chase,
Still in a tree did end their race.
Apollo hunted Daphne so,
Only that she might laurel grow.
And Pan did after Syrinx speed,
Not as a nymph, but for a reed.
—Andrew Marvell, The Garden

The pride of the peacock is the glory
*   of God.*
The lust of the goat is the bounty of
*   God.*

The wrath of the lion is the wisdom
*   of God.*
The nakedness of woman is the
*   work of God.*
*   —William Blake, The Marriage*
*   of Heaven and Hell*

The horn of the celestial goat
*   touches the sun.*
*   —Dante, The Divine Comedy*

Thou damned and luxurious
*   mountain goat.*
—William Shakespeare, Henry V

What was he doing, the great god
*   Pan,*
Down in the reeds by the river?
Spreading ruin and scattering ban,
Splashing and paddling with hoofs
*   of a goat,*
And breaking the golden lilies
*   afloat*
With the dragon-fly on the river.
*   —Elizabeth Barrett Browning,*
*   A Musical Instrument*

83

T he appearance of Capricorn, the goat sign, begins the western year. Its name in Latin means "the horn of the goat." The goat is often depicted with the tail of a fish, which variation probably originated with the Babylonians. The Sumerians gave the constellation a ram's head and identified it with Ea, whose ideogram meant "home of the waters," and indeed Capricorn inhabits that part of the heavens called the Sea. Ea was a god of land and water, so the depiction of a goat with a fish's tail is appropriate. The Sumerians call the constellation "goat-fish," and it is represented on Kassite boundary stones. The Aztecs, too, associated it with a horned fish, Cipactli.

The Zulus saw Capricorn as the sheep of the sea, and consider people born under this sign to be perfectionists, fanatical about self-improvement and sometimes about improving others. They can make good teachers. The related tale tells of Ntintilili the seal, who criticized God the Father as he was creating the world, suggesting that he give everyone four eyes instead of two and make the animals stronger. She also told him he was wrong to make sunrise and sunset and winter and summer. It was just too confusing, sometimes too light, sometimes too dark, sometimes too warm, and at other times too cold. Finally she objected to God the Father giving everyone genitals because they

would spend all their time making love instead of working, as they should. God the Father felt he had to silence Ntintilili, so he turned her legs into flippers (though he took care to preserve her genitals). He told her Ocean was more patient than he was, so she should go tell him how to run his sea-kingdom.

There is a thirteenth Zulu month, from December 28 to January 6, which is represented by Ukahomo the Whale. Thirteen is a sacred and lucky number for Zulus. This interstitial month is considered the most holy, and many ceremonies are conducted at this time. People born under the sign of Ukahomo the Whale are seers and fortune tellers, and they should serve others by doing sacred work. It is counted as very lucky to be born in this thirteenth month. *Ukahomo* for the Zulus means "the one who knows everything." People born at this time try to become wise and never

find contentment in their search: they know that the quest for wisdom is unending.

The Greeks see the constellation Capricorn as Amalthea, a nymph who provided nourishment to the infant Zeus and made sure that Cronus would not find the child. She had the Curetes (sons of Rhea, the earth mother) and Corybantes dance and make noise to distract the searching Cronus. Upon his ascendance Zeus gave her a horn, the cornucopia, or horn of plenty, which provided a never-ending supply of delicious things to eat and drink. In some versions of the myth, Amalthea was a she-goat.

Sometimes Capricorn is identified with Pan, in various myths the son of Amalthea, who took the shape of a goat when he was terrified by the monster Typhon. Other myths say Pan was the son of Hermes and a nymph, or of Hermes and Penelope, or possibly even the collective son of

85

OPPOSITE: *The Young Bacchus* (1620), BY GUIDO RENI (1575–1642), OIL ON CANVAS. PAN, DIONYSUS, AND BACCHUS ARE ALL LINKED IN THE FIGURE OF THE CONSTELLATION CAPRICORN, THE "GOATISH" SIGN. (PALAZZO PITTI, FLORENCE)

BELOW, LEFT: THIS MARBLE STATUE BY GIAN LORENZO BERNINI (1598–1680) DEPICTS THE GOAT AMALTHEA WITH THE CHILD JUPITER AND A FAUN. CAPRICORN CAN BE SEEN TO REPRESENT THIS BENEVOLENT GOAT-MOTHER, WHO NURSED ZEUS. (GALLERIA BORGHESE, ROME)

BELOW, RIGHT: ALTHOUGH TRADITIONALLY SHOWN WITH A SYRINX, OR PIPE, THE SYLVAN GOD PAN IS DEPICTED IN THIS FRESCO PLAYING THE LYRE. (VILLA OF THE MYSTERIES, POMPEII)

all her suitors. Pan was a lusty god of shepherds, and vastly enjoyed chasing (and ravishing) nymphs. He invented the panpipe, or syrinx, which was named for the nymph who escaped his embrace by changing herself into a reed. Another fleeing nymph, Pitys, changed herself into a pine tree, so he carried the thyrsus; a branch with a pine cone, to commemorate her. Pan was often identified with Dionysus, to whom the thyrsus was also sacred. Dionysus thus was a patron of this constellation, and

ABOVE: IN *PAN AND THE NYMPH SYRINX* (1657), BY MICHEL DORIGNY, SYRINX FLEES THE GOATSMAN. (LOUVRE, PARIS)
OPPOSITE: THIS SIXTEENTH-CENTURY FRESCO BY GIOVANNI M. FALCONETTO SHOWS JUPITER AND PAN IN FRONT OF HADRIAN'S VILLA. (PALAZZO ARCO, MANTUA)

much wine is drunk during January in Greece, in particular to celebrate the rebirth of the sun after the winter solstice.

Pan could spread panic (named for him) throughout an army, and Greek myths suggest that he helped the Greeks during the war against the Persians in this manner. To commemorate his aid, the sylvan god asked for temples to be built. Pan also helped the gods in their fight against the Titans by blowing into a conch shell. Some versions of this event state

that he was given a fish's tail to celebrate his role in this fight.

Pan was a grotesque figure, a man from the waist up and a goat from the waist down, with horns on his head and cloven feet. His image was an obvious target for such Christian zealots as Eusebius, a holy father who lived in the fourth century A.D., who transformed the god into a manifestation of the devil. Greek spirits, called *daimones*, were likewise later interpreted as demons. But in antiquity Pan was considered a pleasant and amusing god (except to some of the women he hunted); in fact, some see the etymology of Pan ("all") to have come from the fact that

ABOVE: This hand-colored Italian engraving shows the school of the Vestal Virgins. Capricorn was sacred to Vesta, the Roman goddess of the hearth whom the Vestal Virgins served.

he pleased all the gods. This is folk etymology, whereas others see the name as a simple sound like "pa" in "papa." In this way, the image of Pan can be broadened to signify the entire universe.

As mentioned earlier, Cancer and its opposite Capricorn were also considered by Platonists and Chaldaeans as the passageways for souls to go to and come from earth: arrivals via Cancer and departures via Capricorn. The Tyrian philosopher Porphyry (c. 300 B.C.) speaks of these heavenly gates in his essay "In the Cave of the Nymphs." The Romans considered this constellation to be sacred to Vesta, the ancient, much-revered goddess of the hearth.

Interestingly, Christians came to consider this the birth date of Christ, just as the ancient Persians considered it the birth date of the god Mithras.

Hindus call this constellation *Nakshatra-Abhijt*, "the victorious." In China it was *Nieu*, "the ox." The Hebrews took this as an emblem for the tribe of Naphtali: "Naphtali is a hind let loose" and Capricorn in this case is construed as a deer. Other Hebrews saw it as representing the tribe of Dan. And some Christians thought Capricorn represented the apostle Simon.

Capricorn (December 22 to January 19) is a cardinal earth sign and its ruling planet is Saturn. Its plant is a poplar tree and its gems are garnet and tourmaline. Its colors are brown, black, gray, and green. The most compatible signs are Virgo, Taurus, Scorpio, and Pisces, but fiery Aries and witty Gemini can provide a good counterbalance to the sometimes dour Capricorn. People born under this sign display some saturnine characteristics, with a tendancy to be loners. They can be fanatics (for example, Joan of Arc), but they generally get what they want because they are extremely persevering. They are ambitious, loyal, passionate, and creative in a systematic way. Like the goat, they are accustomed to scaling heights (they like mountains). They write, organize, and calculate well. Capricorns make good academics, architects, and crusaders, and in general succeed at almost anything that requires hard work. They are frequently accomplished in the areas of music, art, comedy, and storytelling. Notable people born under this sign are Anne Brontë, Pablo Casals, Paul Cézanne, Anton Chekhov, Brian Friel, Henri Matisse, Molière, Isaac Newton, Louis Pasteur, Albert Schweitzer, and the author of this book.

89

Many early cultures such as Persia, Turkey, Syria, and Arabia named this constellation after the goat. Arabs saw it as "the fortune of those who sacrifice," and nanny goats were sacrificed in a festival around December 25.

AQUARIUS

Great God! I'd rather be
A Pagan suckled in a creed
  outworn;
So might I, standing on this
  pleasant lea,
Have glimpses that would make me
  less forlorn;
Have sight of Proteus rising from
  the sea;
Or hear old Triton blow his
  wreathèd horn.
  —William Wordsworth, "The
  World Is Too Much with Us"

When the moon is in the seventh
  house,
And Jupiter aligns with Mars,
Then peace will guide the planets,
  And love will see the stars.
This is the dawning of the age of
  Aquarius.
  —James Rado and Gerome Ragni,
  "Aquarius," Hair

Aquarius is the cupbearer of the classical zodiac, the one who pours water. The Egyptians observed that the Nile flooded when Aquarius dipped his cup into it, causing it to overflow, an annual occurrence vital for continued fertility. Likewise, the Babylonians saw the constellation as a water goddess. In Greek mythology, Aquarius is identified with Ganymede, the beloved of Zeus, who was carried off by his eagle. Ganymede was the fair son of Laomedon or Tros, ancient kings of Troy, and was so attractive that the kings Tantalus and Minos sought his affection. In the end it was Zeus who won out: he made an offer that could not be refused, actually snatching the boy

away. In return, he awarded Laomedon (or Tros) a splendid golden vine and a divine pair of steeds, as swift as the North Wind, their father. It was these steeds that Heracles was promised for sorting out the mess that Hesione got into, due to her father's treachery.

In Euripides' *Trojan Women* the chorus laments that the god's favor shown to one of their princes, Ganymede, was not enough to save the city. There is a poignant contrast between the boy saved by the gods, and the women condemned to suffering.

Zeus' eagle and swan—the latter the form he took to impregnate Leda—are symbols of his power and sexuality.

THE RAPE OF
GANYMEDE, BY PETER
PAUL RUBENS
(1577–1640).
AQUARIUS IS THE
CUPBEARER, A ROLE
GANYMEDE FILLED AFTER
BEING CARRIED OFF BY
ZEUS. (MUSEO DEL
PRADO, MADRID)

Flying penises figure prominently in ancient art from countless cultures.

There is little doubt, at least according to the literary tradition, that Ganymede served Zeus in more ways than one. Robert Graves traced the etymology of Ganymede to *ganusthai medea*, which translated literally means "rejoicing in the genitals" or "virility." In Greece and Rome, homosexuals cited this myth as divine justification for their practice. To this tale ancient homosexuals might have added the stories of Apollo's love for Hyacinthus, Poseidon's for Pelops (whom he also made his cupbearer), and, on the "heroic" level, Heracles' love for Hylas, and Laius' kidnaping of Pelops' son Chrysippus (in direct imitation of Zeus carrying off an unwilling partner). All these abductions of children symbolize the yearning for youth felt by an older partner.

Some of these myths did not have happy endings. When Laius kidnapped Chrysippus, the youth committed suicide from shame. Chrysippus' father cursed Laius, who was Oedipus' father, and thus all Oedipus' troubles began. The curse was that Laius' own son would kill his father; Laius tried to escape his fate by exposing Oedipus at birth, but a shepherd and his wife rescued the child and the curse was eventually fulfilled, as it always is in Greek myths.

Zeus himself may be associated with this constellation even more directly; as the god of thunder—rain and storm—he was the one who watered the earth. There was even an expression in ancient Greek for this seminal act: "Zeus rains."

The constellation Aquarius may represent Hebe, the goddess who also acted as cupbearer to the gods. She was a

THE STATUE *HEBE*, BY ANTONIO CANOVA (1757–1822), SHOWS THE WIFE OF HERACLES AND THE CUPBEARER FOR THE GODS, WHO IN SOME VERSION WAS SUPPLANTED BY THE YOUNG GANYMEDE. (PINACOTECA CIVICA, FORLÍ, ITALY)

daughter of Zeus and Hera, and was given to Heracles as his bride. Her name means "youth," and such is her essence; she is the female representative of the youthful beauty discussed above. Heracles—after he accomplished all his labors, for the most part instigated by Hera—became the mighty goddess' son-in-law. His last three labors were all associated with the conquest of death; his becoming immortal, with "youth" as his bride, certainly crowned these efforts.

A later Greek myth associates this constellation with the story of Deucalion and Pyrrha, the two "good people" saved from the flood sent by Zeus to wipe out wicked humanity, the Greek equivalent of the biblical story of Noah. Prometheus, the benefactor of mankind who stole fire from the gods for man's benefit, told Deucalion, his son, how to build an ark. In this ark Deucalion and Pyrrha braved the storm, which lasted nine days and nights, and finally landed on a mountain in Thessaly. The elderly couple had to repopulate the world, and they were told to throw "their mother's bones" behind them; they rightly guessed that the "bones" were actually stones (Ovid said that this is the reason we are a "stony" race). There is also a play on the Greek words for stone, *laas* (sometimes *laos*), and for people, *laos*. It is the water of the flood that links Aquarius with Deucalion.

The constellation Aquarius is found in the area called the Sea by ancient astronomers. The water gushing from the urn ends in a bright star called Fomalhaut, from the Arabic words *fom al hut*, "the fish's mouth." A fish called the *Piscis Austrinus,* one of the two fish comprising Pisces,

seems to be drinking the whole stream. When the sun is in this constellation, it signals a time of heavy rains.

The Zulus see this sign as a boatman, Usihlenga, and also as Ubembezi, Africa's firebird. When the firebird gets old, it lights two torches and sets its feathers on fire, thereby renewing itself, like the legendary phoenix. A story is told of Mawela, the boatman who ferries the gods across the Milky Way. One day Mawela found a beautiful goddess waiting to be ferried across. This was Nomvula, the daughter of the

LEDA AND THE SWAN, BY PETER PAUL RUBENS (1577-1640). LEDA WAS ONE OF THE OBJECTS OF ZEUS' LUSTFUL FURY; HE TOOK THE SHAPE OF A SWAN IN ORDER TO SEDUCE HER. (GEMÄLDEGALERIE, DRESDEN)

thunder god. She was very sick and was on her way to see. Sompisis, the great sangoma, or shaman, to find out what she could do. Nomvula told Mawela the whole sad story, about how Earth Mother had made a snide comment about the size of her buttocks, and so Nomvula called her a dirty name. Earth Mother changed into the monster Nomhoyi and put a withering curse on her, and the only way the afflicted Nomvula could be cured would be if she could find someone who would be willing to sacrifice everything for her.

Mawela, who was already head over heels in love, offered to help. He didn't know what·he was letting himself in for. He first had to give the sangoma a cow. Then he had to give Nomvula blood. Then he had to kill a savage hippopotamus so that Nomvula could eat its liver. Finally, Mawela had to get Earth Mother to remove the spell, which she said she would do for a sacrifice: his hand, which she would eat when she took the form of the monster Nomhoyi. Mawela did this also, and finally Nomvula recovered. Mawela's hand grew back and Earth Mother said she had

THIS INDIAN PRINT (C.1725) FROM RAJASTHAN, JAIPUR, INDIA, SHOWS THE VEDIC GOD INDRA RIDING AIRAVATA, HIS ELEPHANT. WHEN THE FULL MOON IS IN AQUARIUS, INDRA'S VICTORY OVER DARKNESS IS CELEBRATED. (PIERPONT MORGAN LIBRARY, NEW YORK CITY)

rewarded him because of his faithful love. Nomvula became the boatman's wife, and they are regarded as a god and goddess of love.

The Zulus believe that people born under this sign are idealists and spiritually developed. They wander a lot, and try to rectify the wrongs they encounter in the world. They are not the easiest people to love and understand. They love new things and begin many projects. They are ardent in their pursuit of truth, but they rarely know what they are seeking, another reason for their wandering.

In India, the full moon in the constellation of Aquarius was the occasion for a ceremony conducted to celebrate the sun's victory over darkness (Indra over Vritra). To fortify himself, Indra drank the divine drink, *soma*, which is identified with Chandra, the moon. This time of year in India is associated with monsoons. Giuseppe Maria Sesti identifies Aquarius with Trita Aptypa, the god of waters who prepared the *soma* for Indra. Trita Aptypa is identified with Triton, the original sea-god of Greece. The constellation is also seen as Catabhishaj, the one hundredth medical doctor under Varuna, the god of order.

There is a Peruvian legend that calls this constellation the Mother of the Waters. The Sumerians also linked it with the month called Shabatu, or the "curse of the rain." The Hebrews associated Aquarius with the tribe of Reuben, "unstable as water." Arabs, after Mohammed, avoided the anthropomorphic and called this constellation *al-Dalw*, or "the pail of the well." The Christians saw it as John the Baptist, or the apostle Judas, or even Moses, saved by the waters. The Anglo-Saxons called it *se Waeter-gyt*, the "water-pourer."

In China, this constellation is also associated with water. Along with Sagittarius, Capricorn, and Pisces it was the early serpent, or turtle, *Tien Yuen*, linked with the emperor Tchoun Hin, who

THE BAPTISM OF CHRIST, BY PIERO DELLA FRANCESCA (1415–1492). JOHN THE BAPTIST IS ASSOCIATED WITH AQUARIUS. (NATIONAL GALLERY, LONDON)

had a flood during his reign. This is also the sign of the Rat, which shares the ideograph for water. However, the Chinese associated stars in this constellation with other formations as well, including "the camp with entrenched walls," "the empty bridge," "the imperial guard," and "the tomb."

95

In all of these myths the sun is viewed as caus-ing rain when it is in a certain place in the sky in relation to the stars. The myth-making mind often created cause-and-effect relationships between two coincidental events: if it is spring when the swallows come back to Capistrano, and the swallows do not come back to Capistrano, there will be no spring. The pecking groundhog on Groundhog's Day functions in the somewhat same way. In Marcel Camus' film *Black Orpheus* (1959), the hero sings the sun up, a poetic reference to these ancient beliefs.

In the year 2000, the sun will enter this constellation on the day of the spring equinox, March 20. At that point Earth will enter the age of Aquarius. People under the sign of Aquarius are considered amiable idealists and dreamers,

THE BLACK TORTOISE OF CHINESE ASTRONOMICAL MYTH, FORMED BY SAGITTARIUS, CAPRICORN, PISCES, AND AQUARIUS. (NEAR THE FORBIDDEN PALACE, BEIJING)

who are concerned with humanity and creative change. It is these values that will inform the Age of Aquarius.

Aquarius (January 20 to February 18) is a fixed sign of air, ruled by Saturn. Its plant is ivy, and its flower is violet. Its gems are amethyst and sap-phire, and its colors are blue and green. Signs compatible with Aquarius include Libra and Gemini. Aquarians work well with charities, are active in human rights, and are good inventors, healers, and intellectuals. Famous people born under this sign include Bertolt Brecht, Robert Burns, Colette, Charles Darwin, Seamus Deane, Thomas Edison, Galileo, James Joyce, Abraham Lincoln, Edouard Manet, Wolfgang Amadeus Mozart, Franz Schubert, Gertrude Stein, Virginia Woolf, and William Butler Yeats.

PISCES

’Ιχθύες

The living mother-of-pearl of a salmon
just out of the water

is gone just like that, but your stick
is kept salmon silver.
—Seamus Heaney,
"A Hazel Stick for Catherine Ann," Station Island

Fish got to swim and birds got to fly.
—Oscar Hammerstein II,
"Ol' Man River," Showboat

And here fantastic fishes duskly float,
Using the calm for waters, while their fires
Throb out quick rhythms along the shallow air.
—Elizabeth Barrett Browning,
A Drama of Exile

The final sign of the zodiac is Pisces. In the West, this constellation is considered to be two fishes, joined by a chain. They swim in the part of the heavens called the Sea.

One story related to this constellation concerns the Syrian goddess Derceto, or Atargatis, who is like Aphrodite. Two fishes took a giant egg they found to land, and a dove covered it (doves are also sacred to Aphrodite). The goddess emerged and awarded the fish with immortality in the stars. (Likewise, in the Egyptian canon, when Isis was in labor, a fish helped her and she rewarded

OPPOSITE: *SEMIRAMIS*, BY MATTEO ROSSELLI (1578–1650), SHOWS THE MYTHOLOGICAL QUEEN QUELLING A REBEL-LION IN BABYLON. DERCETO, HER MOTHER, ABANDONED HER BY TRANSFORMING HERSELF INTO A FISH. (VILLA DELLA PETRAIA, FLORENCE)

him by placing him in the stars.) Another story about Derceto is that she offended Aphrodite, whose punishment was to make her fall in love with the mortal priest Siron, who fathered Semiramis on her. When Derceto realized what she had been forced to do, she angrily first cas-trated and then murdered Siron, and abandoned her daughter in the desert; she herself dove into a lake in Palestine and became a fish. The Syrians represented her with the upper body of a woman and the lower body of a fish, making her one of the first mermaids.

The Babylonians called the northern fish *Anunitu*, "lady of the heavens." This may have inspired the myth that has Aphrodite and her son, Eros, taking the form of fish to escape from the frightful monster Typhon, much as Dionysus took the form of a goat to escape the same monster. Other versions of this myth recount that the sea-born goddess and her son were rescued by fishes.

The Arabs generally see this constellation as a fish that swims in the river of stars flowing from Aquarius' urn. The Hebrews assigned this joint constellation to the tribes of Simeon and Levi.

The Zulus tell a romantic story about this constellation, which for them is two dolphins named Koko and Kukuku. When the Earth Mother was creating Earth she accidentally dropped the pearl of life while being chased by a vicious whale in the ocean. She was at a loss: what would Earth be without life? She called on the two dolphins Koko and Kukuku to help her. They searched high and low and finally found the precious pearl. Koko carried it in her mouth and they sped toward Earth Mother, who was weeping on the Isle of Loneliness. Unfortunately a many-headed monster called Mningi spied the two dolphins and made plans to eat them. When the dolphins saw him coming, they cried piteously to Earth Mother but she was asleep. Her faithful owl heard them and sent a carp named Ntambi to get the pearl safely from Koko, which he did, and returned it to Earth Mother. Mningi ate one of the dolphins and the other said it could not live without its mate:

Mningi was glad to oblige. Earth Mother could not save their lives, but at least she could commemorate the lovers in the heavens.

These Africans believe that people born under this sign are courageous, dedicated to achieving their goals, and committed to preserving their accomplishments. They are faithful friends and lovers and enjoy company. They can be moody, like the sea. Sometimes they are very suspicious.

One of the symbols of Christ is also a fish, and in fact the acronym of his Greek title spells the Greek word for "fish": *Ichthus* is I*esous* Chr*istos,* th*eou* u*ios, s*oter, or "Jesus Christ, the son of God, our savior." It became the secret sign of persecuted Christians in ancient Rome. Christians identify Pisces with Saint Matthew, the apostle who took the place of Judas, the trai-

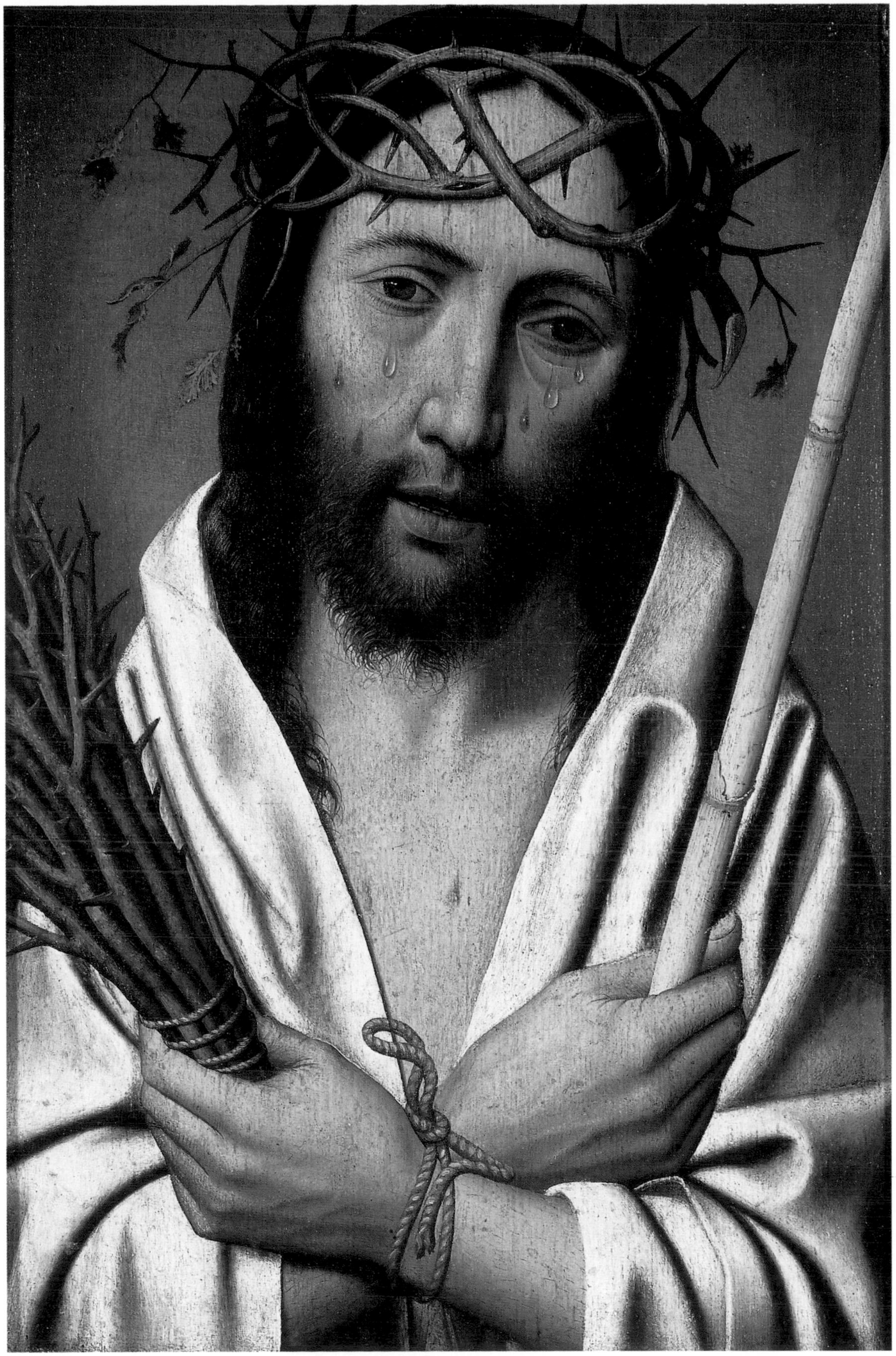

From all the pancultural evidence, the constellation Pisces represented mainly benevolent fish, commemorating a creature that has fed mankind for centuries.

Pisces (February 19 to March 20) is a mutable water sign governed by Neptune, named for the god of the ocean. Its plant is the lilac (colored like some seas) and its gem is, appropriately, aquamarine. Pearls and moonstones are also gems connected with this sign. Its colors, of water and fish, are green and silver. People born under this sign get along well with Capricorn, Scorpio, and Cancer. Pisces are intuitive, sensitive people. They love the water, tend to be emotional, and in fact can be carried away by their feelings; sometimes they are weak-willed and indecisive, and have to work to counteract this tendency. They are fun to be with. They are dreamers and can be creative; these qualities can make them great poets, musicians, composers, writers, seers, healers, prophets, and teachers. They make excellent actors. Outstanding people born under this sign include Elizabeth Barrett Browning, Enrico Caruso, Frédéric-François Chopin, Albert Einstein, Peter Fonda, George Frideric Handel, Michelangelo, Ovid, Auguste Renoir, Arthur Schopenhauer, and George Washington.

tor. This constellation also represents the fish that Christ used to feed the multitude.

To the Chinese, this constellation in the northern corner of the zodiac was called "dark warrior," "residence of the dark emperor," and "the pig." Individual stars were "lightning" and "cloud and rain." This region of the heavens was considered a stormy place, and most Chinese observers associate these stars with the North (though some stars were called Wae Ping, "a rolled screen").

THE MILKY WAY

Across rough seas,
It arches toward Sado Isle—
The River of Heaven.

—Bashô

Before sentiments were recruited on the
    walls
I could hear the constellations
Creak in winter's axle
As I gazed out the window
Towards the New Year bells
That chimed their benisons
Into the lighted houses.
Orion took my fancy most.
    —Seamus Deane, "Send War in Our
        Time, O Lord"

104

Our solar system is part of the Milky Way galaxy, and "galaxy" comes from the Greek *gala*, meaning "milk." As home to the zodiac, the Milky Way merits special attention here.

The band of Milky Way is a huge nebula that covers more than one-tenth of the sky as seen from Earth and contains 90 percent of the known stars. It is in the form of a river that at one point divides into two branches. Some cultures—like the Greek, Egyptian, Arabic, Hebraic, Chinese, and Japanese—called it the River of Heaven, and others—like the Romans, Norse, North American

ABOVE: THIS BRONZE PORTAL DECORATION DEPICTS THE MOTHER GODDESS THALASSA (SEA), OR ASHERAH (WATER), AND GAIA (EARTH) SUCKLING THEIR CHILDREN. THE MILKY WAY IS FREQUENTLY ASSOCIATED WITH THE MILKY OFFERING OF THE UR-MOTHER GODDESS. (SAN ZENO CATHEDRAL, VERONA)

Indians, Eskimos, and Bushmen of Africa—saw it as a highway or path. In many countries it was used to mark seasonal changes. Both the ancient Chinese and Peruvians linked it with the rainy season.

Some Greeks thought the Milky Way was the scorched path left by the foolish and unskilled Phaëthon when he borrowed the chariot of his father, Helius, the sun god. The animals of the zodiac gave the young charioteer a scare—particularly Scorpio, who threatened him with his claws—and his chariot careened off the path. He burnt the stars, creating the Milky Way, and

seared Earth, creating deserts in Africa and blackening the skin of those people too near to his flaming route. The stars and Earth complained so bitterly about the heat that Zeus struck Phaëthon down with a thunderbolt. The unfortunate young man plunged into the river Eridanus, northern Italy's Po River; his grieving sisters were turned into poplars that mourn him for eternity, weeping teardrops of amber. In some accounts, the Milky Way is not the remains of burnt stars but rather sunbeams scattered by the sun's chariot during Phaëthon's mad flight.

Another Greek story suggests that the Milky Way is the former path of the Sun, abandoned by him when he changed his course in revulsion at the spectacle of the grisly banquet served by Atreus to his brother Thyestes: Thyestes' own children.

Greek myth also has it that this wash of stars was formed from Hera's milk, which spurted from her breast when Heracles bit on it—or when she realized whom she was suckling and thrust him from her. One tale suggests that Hermes put the baby, Zeus' son by Alkmene, at Hera's breast when she was asleep, and when she woke up she thrust him away from her in horror. But it was too late: Heracles would be immortal because he had drunk the milk of a goddess. Yet another tale relates that Athena and Hera were walking in Argos and were struck by the baby Heracles' beauty (he had been exposed

PREVIOUS PAGE: THE MILKY WAY, BY PETER PAUL RUBENS, ILLUSTRATES HERA'S SPURTING MILK, WHICH ACCORDING TO SOME MYTHS WAS SAID TO HAVE CREATED THE MILKY WAY. (MUSEO DEL PRADO, MADRID) BELOW: IN THIS RELIEF FROM THE PERGAMON ALTAR (C.180 B.C.), ATHENA FIGHTS GAIA'S (OR RHEA) SONS WHILE GAIA EMERGES FROM BELOW. (PERGAMON MUSEUM, STAATLICHE MUSEEN, BERLIN)

to the elements by his mother, who feared Hera's wrath). Athena urged Hera to suckle the child, which she did; then, after the baby was sated, he bit the nipple. Hera threw the baby down, but once again it was too late: the baby was now immortal. Another version has Hermes at Hera's breast; when the goddess realized she was suckling the bastard son of Maia and Zeus, she hurled him from her, causing her milk to spurt and form the Milky Way.

ANDROMEDA SAVED BY PERSEUS, BY HANS VON AACHEN (1552–1615). PERSEUS' RUSH TO SAVE ANDROMEDA STIRRED UP DUST IN THE HEAVENS AND SO CREATED THE MILKY WAY. (SCHLOSS AMBRAS, INNSBRUCK)

There are other Greek stories that are similar. One was associated with Zeus. His father, Cronus, swallowed all his children because he did not want to be overthrown by them (which is exactly how Cronus had wrested power from his own father, Uranus). Cronus' wife, Rhea, deceived him by giving him a stone wrapped like a baby to swallow instead of Zeus, but he asked her to nurse the "child" just before he swallowed it. She did, and the milk hit the rock in a shower

THIS LATE–HEIAN PERIOD
JAPANESE WORK (1053)
SHOWS THE DESCENT OF
AMIDA AND THE TWEN-
TY-FIVE BODHISATTVAS
TO COLLECT THE SOUL OF
THE DECEASED. MANY
CULTURES SEE THE MILKY
WAY AS A PATH CROSSED
BY PEOPLE WHO HAVE
DIED, AND THE SPIRITS
WHO GO TO COLLECT
THEM. (HOODO
[PHOENIX HALL],
BYODOIN TEMPLE,
KYOTO)

108

THIS ELEGANT CHINESE PAINTING SHOWS A SCENE ON A RIVER. IN THE MILKY WAY, THE CHINESE SEE A RIVER, *TIEN HO*, AS DO MANY OTHER CULTURES.

that then became the Milky Way. Some interpreters believe these myths demonstrate that the ancient mother goddess relinquished some of her knowledge and authority to her patriarchal successors, and that she had to be defeated by trickery because she was so powerful.

Another Greek myth sees Perseus stirring up dust in heaven in his haste to rescue Andromeda, thereby forming the Milky Way. The Milky Way may also be the smoke that rises from Ara, the nearby constellation of "the altar." Homer talks about the smoke that spirals to heaven, a pleasing offering to the gods. According to Babylonian lore, human beings were created to serve the gods and please them with their sacrifices. One of the earliest interpretations was that this was the altar that the Sumerian Utnapishtim built to thank the gods for saving him and his group from the great flood (just as the Christian God later saved Noah). Some Australian aborigines also interpret the Milky Way as smoke.

Some cultures around the Mediterranean and south central Europe saw the Milky Way as straw. The Armenians, Persians, and Hungarians all saw it as straw that was stolen, but dropped during the getaway. The culprit has many names, but the Gypsies are the most popular candidates.

Another popular interpretation of the Milky Way is a heavenly river. Two Mesopotamian versions saw it respectively as "the serpent river" or "the river of the divine lady." The Arabs gave it the name *al-Nahr*, "the river." The Hebrews called it *Nhar di Nur*, or "river of light." Peruvians also called the Milky Way *Mayu*, or "river." The Chinese similarly called it *Tien Ho*, "the heavenly river." In fact, the Milky Way was called just that in a famous poem from *She King*, by the emperor Seuen, who lived in the eighth century before Christ: "Vast is this Milky Way,/ Making a brilliant figure in the sky."

The Japanese elaborated on the image of the Milky Way as a river, calling it "the silver river" and claiming that the fish of the river were frightened by the crescent moon because they took it for a fishhook. Their fear caused them to leap up, making the entire river flash with silver. In Sanskrit the Milky Way was called *Akash Ganga*, "bed of the Ganges." Shepherds said this was a Great River, and the stars around it sheep, with the star Capella the shepherd. Ottawa Indians thought that the Milky Way was the muddy bottom of a river stirred up as a turtle swam along the bottom. This is also a river, according to Platonists and Chaldaeans, by which the souls of the dead enter the afterlife, or reenter Earth, through the gates of Sagittarius and Gemini, or Capricorn and Cancer.

109

The stellar figures of the Weaver (the star Vega in the constellation Lyra) and the Shepherd (Altair in Aquila) at the time of the Maiden's Festival in China, or Tanabata in Japan, use this river to meet once a year, on the seventh night of the seventh month, to fulfill their hopeless, yet eternal, love. Other lovers have used this as a bridge to meet, namely Zulamith and Salami:

They toiled and built a thousand years
In love's all powerful might:
And so the Milky Way was made—
A starry bridge of light.

—*Attributed by R.H. Allen*
to the Finnish Topelius

These lovers were more fortunate than their Japanese counterparts: once they crossed the bridge, they were able to merge in the star Sirius.

THIS VIKING RELIEF IN STONE FROM THE ILE DE GOTLAND ILLUSTRATES THE LEGEND OF VALHALLA, FINAL DESTINATION OF DEAD WARRIORS. HEROES WHO FELL IN BATTLE TRAVELED ALONG THE MILKY WAY TO REACH VALHALLA. (HISTORICAL MUSEUM, STOCKHOLM)

According to the ancient Norse, this was the river traveled by slain warriors on their way to Valhalla. In Teutonic myth, it can be *Wuotanes Weg*, or "Woden's way." Finns saw it as *Linnunrata*, "birds' way." To some North American Indians, the Milky Way was a heavenly road that took ghosts "to the kingdom of Ponemah, to the land of the hereafter." For Hungarians it was a path for warriors to reach heaven when they died in battle. For Patagonians, it was a road for their dead to hunt emus. Italians called it *La Strada di Roma* because they thought that the way to heaven was necessarily through Rome and its church.

In the work of the ancient Greek poet Pindar, the Milky Way was a pathway for the gods. The Siberians saw it as a divine milkmaid or mother goddess, who fed dying souls with her milk and also delivered new souls to babies. The Dutch also call the Milky Way *Vroneldenstraet*, "Madame Hilda's street" (Madame Hilda was an Earth goddess).

Hunters of many cultures saw the Milky Way as a path. In Siberia, some people called this the ski track of a son of a god who chased a divine stag. This stag finally escaped and became the dipper part of the Big Dipper.

There are old English precedents for viewing it as a path, and one Christian interpretation was that it led to the Virgin Mary (an interesting link with Hera). It has also been associated with Jacob's Ladder, and in England, Spain, and France it is sometimes known as "The Way of Saint James." To the Arabs it was the "Pilgrims' road," which led the faithful yearly to Mecca.

Indian traditions linked the Milky Way with snake, and called it the "path of the serpent." It was also thought to be the path of the gods, a royal highway. The Hindus thought that Ariman used it to reach his Elysian throne. Then again, it was known as "the court of God" and "dove of paradise."

The ancient Romans saw the Milky Way as the belt of heaven (*caeli cingulum*) and also as a heavenly highway (*via caeli regia*). Ovid speaks of it as the "High road paved with stars to the court of Jove." American aborigines and Eskimos, along with African Bushmen, called the Milky Way "the Ashen Path," and saw it as the glowing ashes that lit the path for

THIS IS A STONE STATUE OF THE AZTEC GOD OMETECUHTLI, WHO WAS BOTH MALE AND FEMALE AND THE SUPREME CREATIVE DEITY IN THE AZTEC PANTHEON. THE MASK ON HIS HEADDRESS IS OF THE STAR DRAGON, A SYMBOL OF THE MILKY WAY. (MUSEUM FÜR VOLKERKUNDE, BASEL)

the wayfarer returning home. The Incas claimed it was the dust of stars.

As with the constellations, different cultures interpreted this group of stars according to their experience. It was called *Hada Kuttya*, or "The Way of War," in Hungary because their ancestors, who came from Asia, fought their way to Hungary following these stars. In Spain it was called *El Camino de Santiago*, "The Way of Saint James," because this saint was invoked in battle. The Swedes saw it as "Winter Street," and associated it (not surprisingly) with snow. The Celts called it *Arianrod*, "The Silver Street," and then again *Caer Gwydyon*, after the route that Gwydyon took when he tried to find his errant wife. The Egyptians saw the Milky Way as stalks of grain that Isis let drop when she ran away from Typhon. Some of the Chinese called it the Yellow Road. Polynesians thought it was a long, blue, cloud-eating shark.

The Milky Way has frequently been interpreted similarly throughout the world—as a highway, a river, ash, stalks of grain, a spurt of milk. These similarities can be attributed in part by shared human experience, and in part to common human nature. This overarching splendor in the heavens has been the object of man's highest yearnings, particularly for immortality.

Conclusion

There are major differences and amazing similarities in interpretations of the starry heavens throughout the world. In some cases, the similarities can be explained by the patterns of the stars and by the mingling of cultures thanks to travel, commerce, and war. The differences can frequently be attributed to geography: in northern cultures there are stories about snow; in the tropics about water, rain, and floods; and about winds and dust in the mountainous areas. And sometimes the differences reflect the characteristics specific to a way of life: shepherds see sheep and pastures in the stars, while fisherfolk see fish and rivers.

This wonderful chart of the constellations of the northern hemisphere (1469), illuminated and lettered by Giovanni Marco Cinico, is from the *Phaenomena* of Aratus of Soli. (Pierpont Morgan Library, New York City)

The Chinese differ the most from all other cultures in what they see, routinely placing their bureaucracy in the sky, including the various classes from royalty to peasantry. They add gods, animals, things, and abstract principles (such as *Tien Li*, or "heavenly wisdom"). Confucianism mandated an ordered society, which also found its way into the heavens. The Chinese stories connected with the constellations do not tell of violence in the way the stories of western cultures do, but reflect instead the order and control of their society. They

THIS ILLUSTRATION FROM *LES TRÈS RICHES HEURES DU DUC DE BERRY* SHOWS "THE ANATOMY OF MAN." (MUSÉE CONDÉ, CHANTILLY)

have stories of love, such as that of the Weaver and the Shepherd, rather than western tales of rape (as in the tales of Orion and Cygnus, to name just two). There is also an acceptance of the natural and day-to-day: "piled-up corpses" (the star Algol, in Perseus), for instance, or some stars called "heavenly sewer" (the constellation Cetus). Jesuits brought stories to China from the West, and so some constellations have similar names, but if one digs deeply, one usually finds another story that originally explained the constellation. The Chinese zodiac itself, with

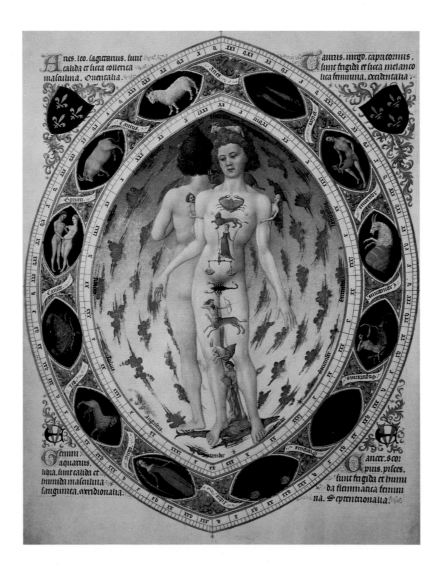

its cycle of twelve animal-years, differs from the western zodiac, which features a different character each month.

The Arabs also had their own interpretations, which tended to become nonanthropomorhic in accordance with Islam after the seventh century A.D. But the Arabic tradition also absorbed some of the common western images, which joined indigenous religious allusions and symbols relating to the paraphernalia associated with living in desert climes.

Native Americans saw tales of the hunt in the stars. They also saw some of their gods, so important in governing the weather, in the heavens. The Chumash, for example, have myths about the Sky Coyote and his yearly gambling match with the Sun. If Sky Coyote wins, Earth flourishes; if the Sun wins, there is drought and death. These tales reflect the importance of the weather, and the type of local animals.

The Polynesians had tales of fishing and voyages; for them, the Milky Way was a big shark. Some African tribes have tales of hunting and animals that are indigenous to their various countries. Indians saw the universe as set first upon a snake, then a turtle, and then four elephants. All of these tales again reflect animals common to those areas.

The Greeks put heroes in the sky (Perseus, for example) and sometimes criminals, along with their punishment (Cassiopeia or Ixion's Wheel, in Ursa Major, for instance). Very human passions are represented in the stars, with tale after tale of anger, rape, and sometimes affection and noble achievement.

Celtic interpretations usually related to heroes—legendary, epic, or even historical figures. Indians placed their gods in the sky, and those associated with myths that ensure human survival, as with Indra's battle over Vritra, representing the triumph of light over darkness. Because gemstones were fairly common in India, they found their way into the heavens as well.

So concludes this brief tour of the heavens. We have seen the struggle of heroes and the loves of men, women, gods, and goddesses commemorated for all time in these shining memorials. Threatening monsters the heroes conquered and the beasts that helped them are still to be seen in stellar form. Antoine de Saint-Exupéry saw the Little Prince in the heavens after the small traveler left Earth, just as many stargazers have seen loved ones whom they have lost. In the heavens, mortal men and women share immortality with the gods and goddesses, their lives celebrated in stellar form.

We can apply Keat's words from "Endymion":

A thing of beauty is a joy forever:
Its loveliness increases; it will never
Pass into nothingness; but still will keep
A bower quiet for us, and a sleep
Full of sweet dreams, and health, and quiet
   breathing.

Like Endymion, we are all lovers of the stars. In the stars, we achieve the ultimate catharsis, setting fears and passions in the heavens so as to overcome them at the same time as they blaze above. Stars can be the loci of prayers and a source of peace and joy. They make us happy to be alive. Looking at the sky, we are never alone, because it is filled with so many friends. For every threat—be it scorpion or bear—there is a hunter or a hero to save us. Our lives unfold with the stars that announce the seasons. There is always a promise of new life and a new dawn, even if sometimes one has to struggle to see it. In the theater of the sky, dramas are replayed every night, with new installments that unfold throughout the year.

The stars are a refutation of our sorrow and a promise of something immortal, if only we can see their promise.

RIGHT: In this beautiful Kangra school painting from 1810, Krishna removes the clothes of some bathing women, recalling an episode in the *Mahabharata* involving the gopis, or cow shepherdesses. The incarnations of Vishnu, including Krishna, are seen in the stars by Indian observers. (Lahore Museum, Lahore, Pakistan)

BIBLIOGRAPHY

Allen, Richard Hinckley. *Star Names: Their Lore and Meaning*. New York: Dover Publications, 1963.

Burkert, Walter. *Structure and History in Greek Mythology and Ritual. Sather Classical Lectures*, Vol. 47. Berkeley, Los Angeles, and London, England: University of California Press, 1979.

Calasso, Robert. *The Marriage of Cadmus and Harmony*. New York: Knopf, 1993.

Detienne, Marcel. *The Creation of Mythology*. Chicago: University of Chicago Press, 1986.

Freud, Sigmund. *The Interpretation of Dreams*. Reprinted in *Great Books of the Western World*. Robert Maynard Hutchins, ed. Chicago/London/Toronto/Geneva/ Sydney/Tokyo/Manila: Encyclopaedia Britannica, Inc. 1987, pp. 135-398.

Graves, Robert. *The Greek Myths*, Vols. 1 and 2. Middlesex, England; New York; Victoria, Australia; Ontario, Canada; Auckland, New Zealand: Penguin, 1986.

Lévi-Strauss, Claude. *Structural Anthropology*. New York: Basic Books, 1963.

Lloyd-Jones, Hugh. *Myths of the Zodiac*. London: Duckworth, 1978.

Krupp, E.R. *Beyond the Blue Horizon: Myths and Legends of the Sun, Moon, Stars, and Planets.* Oxford: Oxford University Press, 1991.

Magee, James Edmund. *Your Place in the Cosmos: A Layman's Book of Astronomy and the Mythology of the Eighty-Eight Celestial Constellations and Registry*, Vols. 1-3. Northfield, Illinois: Mosele & Associates, 1992.

Martin, Martha Evans, and Donald Howard Menzel. *The Friendly Stars: How to Locate and Identify Them*. New York, Dover Publications, 1964.

Ovid. *The Metamorphoses of Ovid*. San Francisco: North Point Press, 1980.

Sesti, Giuseppe Maria. *The Glorious Constellations: History and Mythology*. New York: Harry N. Abrams, Inc., 1991.

119